Voilà!

Effortless French Cookbook

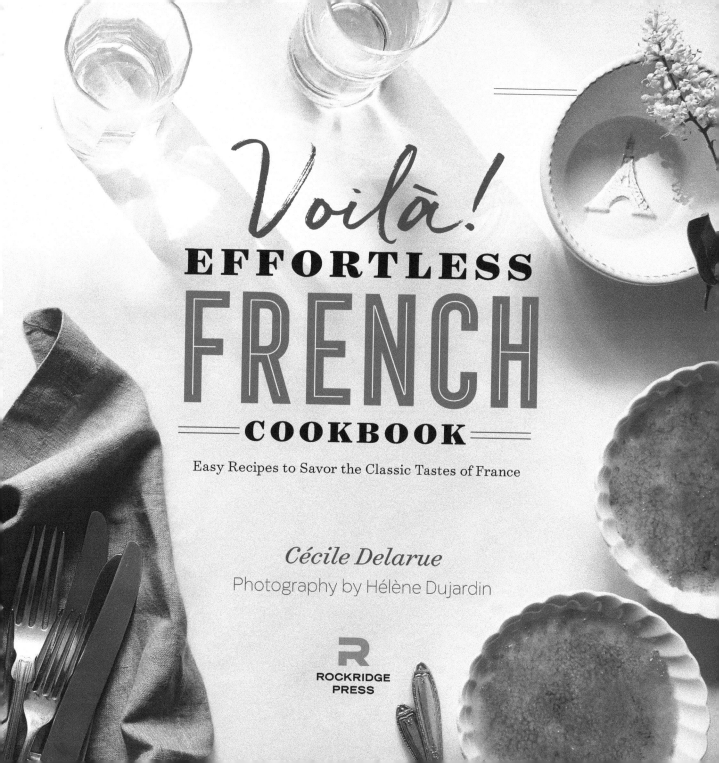

Voilà! EFFORTLESS FRENCH COOKBOOK

Easy Recipes to Savor the Classic Tastes of France

Cécile Delarue

Photography by Hélène Dujardin

R

ROCKRIDGE
PRESS

À ma famille, et à tous les bons
repas à partager ensemble.

To my family, and to all the
good meals to come

Contents

Introduction

I'm not a great chef.

Wait. Maybe that's not the best thing to write when introducing a cookbook.

But it's true. I don't own a Michelin-starred restaurant. I have always stayed away from any exclusive and elaborate cooking classes. And yet, in all honesty, I can still say that I cook very, very good French food.

It's always tricky to talk about French cuisine because of all the clichés that surround it. Yes, it's one of the most elaborate and famous cuisines in the world (and the one that invented the words *chef*, *restaurant*, *menu*, *cuisine*, *café*, *fondant*, and so many more). And yet, it's not necessarily difficult to make. The French food that I cook, for example—and the food more than 60 million people in France cook everyday—is easy to prepare (and is delicious!).

Don't worry if you're a little nervous about making French food—you made the right choice by opening this book. Just be warned: you're going to be surprised by how simple and fast it can be!

I'm French. One hundred percent. I was raised in a village in the Loire Valley a few miles from the Château de Chambord, one of the most beautiful castles in the world. My family has lived there for more than six centuries. They were farmers. Their products—the vegetables my grandparents grew in the garden, the hens and rabbits my grandmother fed every night, the cows that needed to be milked every day at dawn, the wheat my grandfather harvested every summer—took hard work, but these were the best ingredients for what my family thought was one of the most important things: putting something good on the table.

Women in my family have always worked and thus had to squeeze out time to cook for the family and the people who worked at the farm. My parents were the first generation to not be farmers, but every day at lunchtime, my mom made a point to leave the factory where she was working to come home and cook for us. How did these ladies manage to prepare healthy, yummy, satisfying meals in the short time they had? They inherited good, time-tested recipes, and they knew how important it was to share a meal.

French cuisine is not only about preparing and eating amazing dishes. For French people, mealtime is, above all, about sharing something special with others. As my husband, Olivier, always says: "It's the one thing you have to do three times a day, so you better make it great!" And, as you might have noticed if you have ever spent some time at the table with French people, half the conversation actually revolves around food: remembering a great meal you had previously, discussing how you should cook this or that, or describing what you would love to have in the following days!

I cook French food every day. This book contains the recipes I make on a regular basis for my family and friends. They are the dishes I make when I feel nostalgic, the ones I want to pass on to the next generation. From the Boeuf Bourguignon (page 90) I made in college (my first "by myself" dinner—I was so nervous!) to the Gâteau de Savoie (page 205) that I love making for my gluten-free friends in California, all are classic and easy.

As a French expatriate in the United States for seven years now, I have spent hours adapting family recipes to what I can find at my local grocery store, so I hope it will be easy for you too to cook them in your

own kitchen. Please make sure to also follow another great rule of French cooking: cook in season. Using the vegetables and fruits that are naturally growing at the same time of year makes the whole process more interesting, tastier, and healthier—tomatoes that actually saw the sun are much better for you and your palate!

And now, let's get started.

Pour yourself a glass of Chablis and repeat the two best French words after me: "Bon appétit!"

FRENCH COOKING CLASS

CHAPTER ONE

Paris: Where Food Is Everything

Don't bother asking a Parisian what their favorite hobby is—I can tell you right away it's finding the best place to have dinner. Finding the best place for Steak Frites (page 176) or the hidden *petit resto* that serves the best *Pommes Sarladaises* (potatoes sautéed in garlic and butter) is a popular pleasure in Paris. It can also be a time-consuming one!

When you go to a restaurant in Paris, here's what you'll find: You'll first encounter the waiter—he's not grumpy, he's just French—welcoming you with a simple and quick nod, as he is carrying a gigantic tray of seafood—*les fruits de mer*—across the busy room. The menu, hopefully not too overwhelming, consists of a choice of (1) *entrées* (remember, in French the word *"entrée"* means appetizer, as in "entering into the meal"), (2) *plat principal*—main course—usually hot dishes and typically featuring meat or fish, (3) the cheese course, and (4) desserts à la carte. As you settle into the restaurant, you will hear the sound of wine bottles being opened, *"Oui, Chef!"* being yelled from the kitchen, and the people all around you chatting and cheering as they take another bite of their Crème Caramel (page 218).

I could spend many hours watching the exciting life happening at a French bistro. I often wonder how famous writers like Ernest Hemingway or Simone de Beauvoir could ever have focused on their writing in these buzzing scenes where they are said to have written their masterpieces.

There's a reason why the French gastronomical meal has been included in the UNESCO Representative List of Intangible Cultural Heritage of Humanity. Eating is an important and meaningful moment! A meal should be prepared with the best fresh and in-season ingredients, and offered in different courses, always the same and in the same order. First the entrées—the appetizers (usually vegetables, small portioned salads); then a plat principal—the second and most consistent course (usually warm and usually featuring meat or fish); then cheese; and finally dessert.

Just hearing the whole accumulation of different dishes could make some people gain weight! But keep in mind that, like with their wine, the French are careful when they eat. You will often hear in French the important phrase *avec modération*—with moderation. A pinch of this, a bite of that, small portions and big pleasures—that's what French food is all about!

The French Make It Look So Easy

There is a phrase you will hear all the time when you have been invited to a French table for dinner: *"Oh, j'ai fait ça vite fait bien fait, à la bonne franquette."* ("I fixed it very quickly, it's a very no-fuss dinner.") Don't think that your host is just being modest: it's true! Yes, there's a whole feast on the table with appetizers and main courses and the smell of a chocolate cake in the oven. But it didn't take that long: most of the time, it is just a question of combining the right ingredients together, and using very easy techniques to create the meal. In fact, an emphasis on simplicity has been a part of the French culinary tradition for centuries.

Finding a way to throw a delicious dinner party with little time and not that much in the fridge is like a national sport. French people will spend a good amount of time sharing their tricks with their friends on how to make the best last-minute dinner (although you might run into trouble if you ask for an exact recipe—as my mother always says when I ask how much flour to use when making her clafoutis recipe: *"Eh bien,"* she says, *"au pif!"* ("Use your nose!") And when I press her: "Well, you know, just the right amount!" Now you know how hard this book was to write: try and translate "just the right amount" into tablespoons!

EAT MORE LIKE THE FRENCH
1. BE SIMPLE

Don't try to add too many tastes to your dish. Respect the effort of the people who made the ingredients you are using, and never hide their natural tastes by adding other covering flavors. Cooking is like putting on makeup. You only need to enhance what you already have.

You learn French cooking by cooking French food. Once you have basic instructions, you can add a pinch of this or a tad of that, and make the recipe your own. Of course, there is a very elaborate and incredible side of French cuisine, the one you have to learn for years and work extremely hard to be able to master, but you don't have to win the Olympic marathon to enjoy running! What's most important is to learn the basics. Trust me, even the great chefs at the famous restaurants in Paris long to go home and just eat a Blanquette de Veau (page 95) like their grandmother used to make, or the omelette au jambon their father used to flip on Saturdays. *Oui,* French cuisine is easy: if more than 60 million people can cook French recipes every day (while having jobs and kids and crazy lives just like Americans), then you can, too! After you have learned the basics, the rest will become effortless.

Flavors from Home and Abroad

To fully understand why French cuisine has such high quality, look at a map of the country. France has been blessed with a geographical variety that includes regions with yearlong growing climates and rich soil. From the Mediterranean Sea to the green valleys of Normandy, French agriculture has long flourished, and it has produced some of the best ingredients in the world. Great pastures that feed great cows that make great milk that in turn make great cheeses. We call this relationship between the food and the characteristics of its production *terroir*. It's a very important part of what makes French cuisine so good.

Because of France's many climates and regional food specialties, sometimes it is said that the country is actually divided in two halves—the first half, the North, cooks with butter, and the second, the South, with olive oil. But in fact, each region has its own traditions—Normandy and Brittany love butter and cream (Poulet à la Normande [page 166] is cooked in cream, for example, and the crêpes and galettes use butter). But in the southwestern regions, they are often very keen on eating all things duck, from foie gras to Salade Landaise (page 66), and duck fat is often used instead of butter (even to fry "French" fries). Blessed with great soil and delightful wines, Burgundy is the mother region for dozens of classic French dishes, such as Boeuf Bourguignon (page 90) and Gougères (page 44).

As you'll see in the different recipes in this book, neighboring countries have also had a great influence on French menus: southeastern, Provençale, and Niçoise cuisines (Salade Niçoise [page 68] and Daube Provençale [page 91], for example) have a lot of similarities with meals associated with their Italian neighbors (some areas of this part of France belonged to Italy until 1860). Just try to make the recipe for Pissaladière (page 85) and see why the inhabitants of Nice, where it originated, think they invented the pizza first. In the southwestern part of France, Spain is never far—with the Basque Country being both in Spain and in France, most of the recipes from this region are the same on both sides of the border (Poulet Basquaise [page 168], Piperade [page 135], for example). It is also the same along France's eastern border. The traditional foods in Alsace or Lorraine, such as Choucroute Garnie (page 99) or Flammekueche (page 47), are similar to meals you can find in Germany.

Many of the vegetables and fruits that are in our best dishes actually first came to France from other countries. Tomatoes, peppers, corn, and even green beans (even though they are frequently called French beans) first came from the Americas. France, like any country, has also been shaped by its waves of immigration and the way the country colonized others. For example, along with Steak Frites (page 176), one of the favorite dishes of many French people is Couscous—a typical northern African dish that refers not only to the grain, but also the vegetable and meat stew that comes with it.

Even the humble potato—now a staple in French cuisine—came to France from abroad. Did you know for example that the Hachis

EAT MORE LIKE THE FRENCH

3. EAT AT A TABLE

Always. Together. With no screen. Take the time to enjoy a delicious meal with the ones you love. *C'est ça la vie.*

Parmentier (page 184), France's equivalent of Shepherd's Pie, was named after the French noble who convinced King Louis XV to use potatoes as a major food source? The new root vegetable had just come from America and nobody wanted to try it, even though France was suffering from a famine. But when the king decided to have his Royal Guard plant a field of potatoes, the Parisians went to steal some at night, thinking they were some kind of treasure. And that's how the famine ended in France!

And then there's the whole idea of *grandeur*. To establish itself as one of the most important countries in the world, France has always tried to show its power through excellence: with its great castles, its influential fashion trends, its elaborate gardens . . . and its food, too. In the past, for example, French kings would order decadent buffets to impress foreign heads of state or even their enemies. *C'est comme ça*, as the French say. It's just in our blood. Like the character of Asterix, the French comic strip hero, who completed a "tour de France"—but not the famous "Tour de France" with a bike. Instead, he toured the country tasting local cuisines—a real Frenchman's dream!

EAT MORE LIKE THE FRENCH

4. EAT PETIT,
I.E., EAT WITH MODERATION

It's not how much you serve—it's how good it is. Small portions, great pleasure. Try and serve three courses, with a simple appetizer first (crudités, such as Carottes Rapées [page 55] or Céleri Rémoulade [page 54] or a soup, for example), then the main course, then dessert. You stop the hunger with vegetables, then you go on to more elaborate and calorie-rich courses.

It's Not a French Meal Without Wine

It's impossible to imagine a French meal without a nice bottle of wine on the table. It's not about getting drunk. It's about adding a little flavor and pleasure to the moment. Doctors all over the world have heard about the French paradox—the strange scientific discovery that although French people eat fatty foods and regularly drink wine, we have a lower rate of heart diseases. Drinking is something you are taught to love in moderation, even at a very early age—when I was 10, our family doctor told my parents they should start teaching me the different tastes of wine. "Just a tiny sip, along with an explanation,"

The Art of the Cheese Plate

Le plateau de fromages! It's always a very solemn moment during a French meal. You're at the restaurant; you've already had an *entrée* (or as the Americans say, an appetizer) and a *plat de resistance* (or as the Americans say, an entrée!), maybe a few bites of *salade en vinaigrette*; you think you're full . . . and then it arrives. Gigantic, usually held on a tray and full of different shapes, colors, and smells. Cheese plates can be, at some Michelin-starred restaurants for example, overwhelming. My brother, who is a waiter, used to have nightmares whenever he started at a new restaurant. He would dream he couldn't remember the names; or didn't offer them in the right order! There's a whole etiquette around cheese culture. Of course this might not be surprising, in a country where there are around 1,200 types of cheese!

But don't let this scare you: preparing your own *plateau de fromages* is actually pretty easy—even more so if you have a good cheesemonger to help you. The idea is to offer a good and varied selection of cheeses—they should all be different in shape, taste, texture, and flavor—with at least three different types (although as many as five or six for a dinner party of six people is typical).

You should have at least one hard cheese (such as a Comté or Beaufort for the "cooked" cheeses;

Reblochon, Cantal, Morbier, Ossau Iraty for the "non-cooked" cheeses), one soft cheese with rind (Brie, Camembert, Saint-Marcellin, Munster, Pont-l'éveque), one bleu cheese (Roquefort, Fourme d'Ambert, Bleu de Bresse), and one goat cheese (Sainte Maure, Valencay). To this, you can add a fresh cheese or a hard cheese that has a different color, like my beloved Mimolette—this beautiful orange cheese was banned by the FDA a couple of years ago, but it is now back in the United States!

Take the cheeses out of the fridge at least an hour before serving, and place them in a circle, the softest and freshest at the beginning; and the stinkiest at the end!

he said. It's hard to believe, but I had never heard about binge drinking until I was 21 and spent a summer in America studying at UCLA where I watched in shock as students around me got drunk on anything they could find!

Of course choosing the right wine can seem totally overwhelming. But as with anything else, you have to keep it simple. Try to think about what you are going to eat and what kinds of tastes you want to add to the mix. Wine is like adding another spice to a dish—it should complete the food, and highlight its best features. The general rule is that you should always drink red wine with meat and cheese, and white wine with fish—but of course, there are as many exceptions.

My best advice: Go to a real wine dealer, and tell them what you are cooking and what kind of wine you have enjoyed in the past. Talking about what you love and anticipating enjoying the flavors is half the pleasure of drinking it in the first place!

You should also note that French people very rarely classify wines by grape variety (chardonnay, merlot, etc.), but prefer to rank them by the area where the wines are made. You order a Sancerre, a Bourgogne—never a cabernet sauvignon or a chardonnay: it's the location and the tradition that make the taste, not the grapes chosen. Most French people don't even know what types of grapes are used in a Bordeaux, for example, but they can tell the difference between wines from the villages that make Bordeaux wines, from Saint Estèphe to Saint Julien. And anyway, most wines include a combination of different types of grapes.

There are great wine dealers in the United States, and they all talk about wine the French way, just like the Italians or the Spaniards do, by the way: by location. And if you explain what you're cooking, they will be able to help you choose the most appropriate wine.

As for me, as soon as I find a nice red wine I love and trust, I buy a whole case so that I always have the right kind at home, and so I can share it with the friends who invite me for dinner. Here is a quick list of the five must-haves to always keep around your home.

1. *Un Vin Blanc:* A nice mineral white wine is great to drink with fish or other seafood (such as Moules Marinières [page 152]) but also with a nice Flammekueche (page 47). I love Gewürztraminer, from the Alsace region, particularly the *vendanges tardives* (Gewürztraminer grapes are harvested much later than usual, and the wine is much sweeter). But my favorite white wines come from the Loire Valley, where I grew up. These include Vouvray and Montlouis wines, both of which are great as an apéritif or alongside goat cheeses.

2. *Un Vin Rouge:* Red wine is, of course, *obligatoire* in a French wine cellar, and up until 1952 it was even offered in school cafeterias! It's always great to choose a nice Bordeaux (try and get a "second vin," the less expensive version from the best châteaux—the castles where the most exclusive Bordeaux wines are made—or a great Bourgogne (Nuits Saint Georges never fails). But for more unusual options, and often cheaper, you can also find great Beaujolais (although *NEVER* the Beaujolais Nouveau—please, it is just a marketing trick). But try a Julienas or a very romantic Saint Amour! Or perhaps a wine from the Loire Valley (long live the Chinon and Bourgeil—two excellent designations—the latter being my favorite as my grandfather used to make it). These wines are very versatile, full of nice fruity flavor, and always less expensive. Some of them are also *vins tranquilles*, organic wines made in a very traditional way, with subtle and generous taste.

3. *Un Vin Rosé:* Rosé wine is the summer wine par excellence. It wasn't always a sign of good quality, but it is now much better. Enjoy a Côtes de Provence with grilled meat and Ratatouille (page 133)!

4. *Un Champagne:* There's only one real champagne and it's French. And you should always have a bottle in the fridge! Serve it before the

EAT MORE LIKE THE FRENCH

5. NO SNACKING

The French seem to eat a lot at the table because that's the only place they eat. Kids usually have a snack in the afternoon, around 4 p.m., called *le quatre heures* or *le goûter.* But after four, you have to wait for dinner!

meal as an apéritif or for dessert. This is the best wine for celebration, and it is also a versatile wine to drink throughout the whole meal. Give me a glass of champagne and an aged Mimolette cheese for example, and we'll be friends forever!

5. *Un Cidre:* Apple cider is a great tradition in the western parts of France. It is also often the first taste of alcohol for French kids. It's not very high in alcohol content, and it goes very well with crêpes. It's far less sweet than the American nonalcoholic version, and it is great served with crêpes and galettes (Galette des Rois [page 220], for example) but also with foie gras or roasted chicken.

Le Cordon Bleu?

It's a dream shared by millions: One day, when the time is right, you'll buy a plane ticket, leave everything, and go to Paris where you will eat croissants on the steps of Notre Dame and take a cooking class at Le Cordon Bleu. But you don't need to be Audrey Hepburn in the movie *Sabrina* to learn how to break an egg or make a great Soufflé au Fromage (page 51)! And you don't need to go to Le Cordon Bleu, either (the school is not very well known in France or among professionals there). There are plenty of cooking school options, the most celebrated being l'Ecole Ferrandi, where you can learn how to master French pastry or bistronomy with the best "MOFs"—i.e., chefs and pâtissiers who won the prestigious and extremely selective Meilleur Ouvrier de France competition. Some of the best Michelin-starred chefs also have their own cooking classes or workshops—I suggest Anne-Sophie Pic's, l'École Scook, in Valence.

But one doesn't need to go to a fancy class to learn how to master the basics of French cooking. If you had the luxury to go to France, I think the best way to learn "real" French cuisine would be just to spend some time with a French family or with French friends. This is how I learned: from my family. But also just with good, simple cookbooks. Start making some basic recipes, just like the kind in this book, and *voilà!*

Ingredients

Ask any French chef—it's not about the technique—it's about the recipe and the ingredients. Every good meal starts with what you find at the farmers' market or, more generally, what is in season. French food was created by people who had to put something on the table with what they found in the garden or in the fields nearby. And it's important to keep to this rule, however easy it is now to find strawberries in winter. The seasons decide what's on the menu and mark a time for celebration, too—Pot-au-feu (page 93) is for winter, when leeks and turnips are everywhere; Ratatouille (page 133) is for summer, when zucchini and ripe tomatoes flourish.

When grocery shopping, try not to have a definite recipe in mind: My uncle Bernard, a great chef and an important teacher for me, told me to first go and see what's there. What looks good and ripe on the shelves? What piece of meat looks best at the butcher counter? Start there, and then see what recipes include those ingredients. It's so much more creative!

Going to the farmers' markets in France can be an amazing experience: beautiful produce everywhere, merchants yelling that they have the best sausage in town. *C'est magnifique!* It's a pleasure to see how farmers' markets are growing everywhere in the United States, and this beautiful trend is expanding even more! You should take advantage of the markets in your area to find the freshest produce. Also, try to go for the best quality food when you can, even if it is a bit more expensive: better to have a great hormone-free and pasture-raised piece of beef once than a cheap burger twice.

Here are 10 ingredients that you'll see in the recipes in this book and that I try to always have in the kitchen.

1. *Moutarde de Dijon:* Mustard is very important in French cuisine. It's used in many recipes for sauces or to cook meat (it's also my secret ingredient in quiches . . . I spread some on the crust). It's easy now to find Maille mustard in the United States. Make sure it's made in France—in Dijon—and always put it on the table when you serve meat!

2. *Cornichons:* A great snack and the perfect companion to a plate of charcuterie, grilled meat, or Pot-au-feu (page 93), cornichons are tiny pickles that make everything better. They are used for sauces, such as rémoulade. Always have some in the fridge, and try to buy a French-made variety (with no sugar added, ever!).

3. *Beurre:* Butter in France is a delight to eat just on its own, spread on a baguette for example. It has much more color and taste than the typical butter does in the United States. Try and buy European-style butter, or, better, imported French butter. The best are made in Normandy or Charentes. My favorites: Beurre Bordier or Beurre de Baratte, which is exported by my friend Rodolphe Le Meunier, who was named world's best cheesemonger, and is sold in the United States.

4. *Crème Fraîche:* This is a major ingredient for French desserts but also savory dishes. It's not sour cream! For one thing, crème fraîche is much sweeter. Should you have trouble finding it, you can replace it with Mexican crema or whipping cream. I always have on hand the ultra-high-temperature-pasteurized (UHT) shelf-stable whipping cream.

5. *Vinaigre de vin:* Wine vinegar, preferably red wine, is the basis of French dressings, but it is also used in other recipes and techniques,

Herbs

Les fines herbes—fresh herbs—are important in French cuisine. They are what give the flavor and special perfume that make our meals different. They've been used for centuries, if not millennia: back in the eighth century, official documents show that King Charlemagne ordered that thyme, rosemary, and tarragon be planted and grown all over the kingdom for medical and kitchen use.

The most famous use of French herbs is called a "bouquet garni." It's a bundle of herbs used in a lot of classical French dishes, such as *plats à mijoter*—dishes that simmer for a long time (like Pot-au-feu [page 93], Boeuf Bourguignon [page 90], broths, etc.). There's always thyme and laurel in it, plus another herb of your choice, usually parsley, rosemary, sage, or celery leaves.

Here's a trick to always have a bouquet garni ready: Take the green part of a leek (the part you usually throw away). Cut it into 3-inch pieces. Inside each leaf, place a branch of thyme, a laurel leaf, and a branch of parsley (these are examples—you can use whichever herbs you like best). Tie the bundle with a kitchen string. You can then freeze them in a resealable bag and take them out whenever you need them.

THE FIVE HERBS YOU NEED TO COOK FRENCH FOOD

Thyme: It's in the bouquet garni, and in hundreds of French recipes. Thyme is great on grilled meat as well and is also used a lot as a medicinal herb. Drinking thyme as an herbal tea, along with honey, is great when you have a cold or the flu.

Laurel: I always have a pack of dried leaves to add to a soup or a dish.

Parsley: Fresh parsley is used a lot in crudités, the raw salads that are often the first course in a French meal. I also love it sprinkled on top of red meat that has just come out of the pan.

Chives: Minced *ciboulette* is in a lot of recipes, it is at its best raw.

Mint: Fresh mint is very useful in desserts (strawberries and lemon juice and mint make a great summer treat), but also in savory recipes, as you will find in this book. (A small secret from me to you: I sometimes add mint to my bouquet garni!)

like poaching eggs. Another classic is *vinaigre à l'échalote*—red wine vinegar with shallots.

6. *Wine:* Always have a bottle of inexpensive red wine in the pantry. It's great to make last-minute Boeuf Bourguignon (page 90)! Having an inexpensive white wine on hand can also be very useful.

7. *Espelette pepper:* These red peppers grown in the French Basque region are the perfect spice in a lot of dishes, from Poulet Basquaise (page 168) to a chocolate fondant. If necessary, you can replace it with a mix of cayenne pepper and paprika.

8. *Duck fat:* Duck fat is great to cook with (use a teaspoon to fry spinach or kale and you will love your veggies). It is full of flavor, and good for your heart! It's now easier to find at the butcher's or upscale grocery score. A little bit on the expensive side, but you can keep it in the fridge for a long time and most dishes do not use a lot.

9. *Foie gras and duck confit:* Foie gras (duck or goose fat liver) and duck confit are now much easier to find in the United States. Some US farmers are even breeding ducks and geese for this purpose, like Ariane Daguin and her company d'Artagnan on the East Coast, which ships all over the country. Mandatory to make an authentic Cassoulet (page 89)! It's usually canned and preserved in fat, and can be stored for years in the pantry, which makes it the best ingredient for last-minute guests. Keep the duck fat and cook with it later!

10. *Fleur d'oranger:* Orange blossom water is the drop that changes everything. For a last-minute dessert, add a teaspoon to a Pâte à Crêpes (page 32) or pour a tablespoon onto fresh berries. You can find some easily online or in oriental grocery stores.

Equipment

There are two big monuments in Blois, the city in the Loire Valley where I was born: the Château de Blois—a Renaissance castle and one of the historical jewels of the country—and a statue of Denis Papin, a famous inventor. Why is this inventor so important to the inhabitants of the city? Because he, among other great things, invented the pressure cooker—something certainly worth being honored centuries later!

Cooking equipment is very important when you want to cook well, and lots of the most important tools were created in France—from the mandolin for grating and slicing, to the vegetable mill that any French cook needs to make a decent purée. There even used to be a special festival held every year in Paris, Le Salon des Arts Ménagers, where the best new appliances and cooking utensils would be shown to the public.

MUST-HAVE EQUIPMENT FOR YOUR KITCHEN

A good knife: With all the best equipment in the world, you still can't get anywhere without a good knife. Both of my grandfathers always had one in their pocket. A set of Laguiole or Couteaux de Thiers knives are still the best to start a kitchen.

A rolling pin: Preferably wooden. You will need it for Pâte Brisée (page 27)!

A whisk: Having a hand whisk is always useful for omelettes or sauces such as Sauce Béchamel (page 34). A hand mixer is better for pâtisserie in general.

A set of wooden spoons and spatulas: Wood is always preferable to plastic.

A set of good saucepans and a sauté pan: **Preferably nonstick and nontoxic.**

An immersion blender: **My grandmother gave me one for my twentieth birthday. It's still my favorite for making soups!**

A French oven: **More commonly referred to as a "Dutch oven" in North America, this is probably the most expensive piece of equipment on the list, but it's a great investment. A cast-iron pot is the best way to cook all the great one-pot dishes that make French food so festive. It allows food to cook slowly, while protecting the flavors. I personally use one that costs under $50. Otherwise, try to have a heavy-bottom pot.**

Ramekins: **Small ceramic bowls are great for sauces, for dishes like Oeufs Cocotte (page 79), or for desserts like Crème Caramel (page 218).**

Mandolin slicer: La mandoline **is very useful when preparing crudités. These raw vegetable salads all demand that the vegetables be grated or sliced extremely thin.**

A tart pan: **I use mine every other day for quiches or tarts. I prefer one made of steel and with a removable bottom.**

NICE-TO-HAVE EQUIPMENT FOR YOUR KITCHEN

Pressure cooker: **Invented in France, the *cocotte minute* was something of a revolution in the French kitchen, as it allows people to cook traditional recipes much quicker. You can cook a simmered dish in half the time.**

Vegetable mill: Le moulinex, **which is the name of the typical French *moulin à legumes*—vegetable mill—is a stainless steel miracle that is the source of all good purées. It's better than anything else at mashing potatoes, and it's also great when making soups.**

French oven

Vegetable mill

Pressure cooker

Crêpe pan

Tart pan

Ramekins

Crêpe pan: Flipping your own crêpe for the first time is one of the best moments a cook can have, and to do it well you need a pan that has been designed for it. The best crêpe pans are made of blue steel and are not too heavy on your wrist. There is also the famous *billig*—a heavy cast-iron griddle you use at a very hot heat (or its electric version)—that any good family in Brittany must have in their kitchen. Great and easy to use but expensive.

Deep fryer: Frying is not that big in France (fried chicken still seems like a very weird thing to my French friends), but it's nice to have so you can make the best French fries!

Salt and pepper mill: Grinding the best pepper and salt at the last minute can make all the difference in a simple dish. I love the Peugeot mills, which have been made in France for more than a century.

Mortar and pestle: An olive-wood mortar was usually given to all young brides in Provence. It's the best to make aioli and get the maximum flavor out of your garlic and fresh herbs.

Fancy molds: Invest in some Madeleines (page 194) and Cannelés (page 195) molds: once you make these cookies, you will want to make them every weekend!

Techniques

Many of the cooking techniques we use every day were pioneered by French cooks, and many of those techniques are still fundamental today. Just think of the phrase "to sauté vegetables": *sauté* is French for frying in a pan (literally "to jump in the pan"). So if you have sautéed something, you were already cooking *à la Française!* The more you cook, the more you learn how to prepare dishes faster and better. But here are a few basic techniques that will be useful for all kinds of prep work and cooking.

Peeling a tomato: Plunge a tomato into 2 cups of boiling water, leaving it submerged for 1 minute. Meanwhile get a bowl of ice water ready. After 1 minute has passed, place the tomato into the ice water. Leave for another minute. The skin should be easy to take off.

Peeling baked beets or boiled potatoes: Wrap the baked beet or boiled potato in a kitchen towel. Rub the towel against the skin. It should peel off easily.

Poaching an egg: In a saucepan, boil 4 cups of water and add 2 tablespoons of red wine vinegar. Break the egg into a ramekin. When the water begins to boil, lower the heat until the water simmers gently, and then softly drop the egg into the water. When the egg white begins to congeal, use a spoon to shape into a ball and cook for 2 more minutes. Use a slotted spoon to remove the egg from the pan and place it in ice water or serve immediately.

Making lardons: **Lardons** are a common ingredient in a lot of French recipes. These small pork sticks are usually bought precut at the grocery store in France. To make them yourself, buy bacon that is cut into thick slices (about ¼-inch max in thickness) and then cut them into ½-inch wide sticks.

Blanching vegetables: The word "blanch" comes from the French word *"blanchir,"* which means "to whiten." This technique consists of slightly boiling the vegetables before cooking them. Plunge the vegetable into boiling water for 2 minutes and then drain. It's a great way to reduce the bitterness of some vegetables.

Buttering a dish: Cooking spray is one of the most horrific inventions! (Okay—I'm sure I'm exaggerating, but I also know you will never find that kind of product in France.) But the fact is, you don't need it and it's full of chemicals. Before baking, just rub some soft butter onto the mold. Or you can melt a tablespoon in the microwave, let it spread evenly in the pan and put it in the fridge to cool down before pouring the cake in it.

Beating egg whites: My mother still has vivid memories of having to *monter les blancs*—beat the egg whites—with just a hand whisk and a lot of muscles: great for your upper body but very hard, too! It's much easier now with electric appliances, but always make sure you add a teaspoon of salt to the whites. First beat slowly, then faster and faster. Always make sure that the egg whites are cold (they are even easier to use after a couple of days in an airtight container in the fridge).

Rolling a piecrust: I make pies or quiches at least twice a week, and I always think how grateful I am to Anne-Sophie Pic, a famous French chef, for her explanation of how to roll a piecrust. All you need are two sheets of parchment paper. Place one sheet on the table, put the crust on it, then place the other sheet of parchment paper on top. Start flattening the crust with the rolling pin, then flip to the other side. Give it a 45 degree turn to the left, roll it out, flip, turn to the left again, roll again, flip, etc., until you get the perfect size and thickness.

About the Recipes

I tried to select the recipes for this cookbook by choosing things I like to cook every day at home and that make me feel like I'm back in France. These recipes are a good representation of what was on the daily menu when I was a child and what's now on the table in my home in California. I'm a working mom, and I love to have recipes that can be prepared in a few minutes and make my family and friends happy. And you will soon discover that *bonne* cuisine can also sometimes mean "fast food" too!

You'll see by flipping through the book and starting to make the recipes that I tried to keep them simple and effortless. There's no list of impossible-to-find ingredients here. I spent a lot of my first years in the United States trying to understand what could be used and bought here, so I know what is available, and I tried to find a replacement for anything that could be tricky to locate outside of France. There are no unusually difficult techniques in the book either. Everything is explained simply. As you'll see, most of the dishes here only take a few minutes to prep, which should give you some time to do the more important things in life, like relaxing and enjoying life with your loved ones!

You will also find useful labels to help you find the best recipe for you, whether you are gluten-free or on a budget. And don't overlook the tips for pairings or the *petits trucs*—little cooking tricks—that I recommend along the way, which will make the recipes and the cooking even easier.

Now, *à vos tabliers,* put your best apron on and let the fun begin!

Bon appétit!

FRENCH BASICS

CHAPTER TWO

"C'EST LA BASE!" is a phrase you'll often hear in a French kitchen. It means, "These are the basic things you need to know."

Here are eight recipes that are very important and used daily by French people. You're going to see how easy they are and how silly it is to buy store-bought mayonnaise or salad dressing when you can make your own in a matter of seconds. Not to mention that making them at home is far healthier (no additives, no preservatives—you source everything!), and also much cheaper.

These recipes are surely part of "French Cuisine 101," and they were all developed through the centuries. They are the building blocks of French cooking: learning them is like learning your ABCs. They are all part of the first lessons learned at culinary school by a cuisinier or pâtissier. But, like everything in this book, they are extremely easy to make. You'll see that many recipes in the other chapters refer to these first eight, whether they are sweet or savory. From Sauce Béchamel (page 34) to Crème Chantilly (page 31), discover how to master the major steps and learn to make them *en un tour de main*—in just the time it takes to wave your hand!

MAYONNAISE

Prep time: 5 minutes

VEGETARIAN · DAIRY FREE · GLUTEN FREE · UNDER 30 MINUTES · CLASSIC

1 egg yolk

4 tablespoons Dijon mustard

1 tablespoon red wine vinegar

1 teaspoon salt

1 teaspoon freshly ground pepper

¾ cup canola, peanut, or sunflower oil

MAKES 1 CUP · This magical sauce has made French cuisine famous all over the world. Some people pretend it was invented in 1757 by the Duke of Richelieu, the infamous opponent of the Three Musketeers. All I know is that it's always better to make sure all your ingredients are at room temperature. And that the made-from-scratch version is 100 times better than the industrial one. And it's easy, too!

1. In a medium bowl, add the egg yolk, mustard, vinegar, salt, and pepper.

2. Whisk vigorously until all the ingredients are well mixed.

3. Slowly add the oil gradually in a thin stream while continuously whisking until it is completely incorporated.

4. The mayonnaise is thick enough when it hangs off the whisk and doesn't drip.

5. Cover and store in the fridge for up to 2 days.

Le Petit Truc This recipe never fails, but in case your mayo doesn't turn out, try adding a second egg yolk or an additional teaspoon of mustard and whisk again. Some also think it works better when you let the mustard and egg yolk mix rest before adding the oil.

VINAIGRETTE

FRENCH DRESSING

Prep time: 3 minutes

VEGAN · VEGETARIAN · DAIRY FREE · GLUTEN FREE · UNDER 30 MINUTES · CLASSIC

---

1 tablespoon red wine, white, or cider vinegar

1 teaspoon salt

2 teaspoons freshly ground pepper

3 tablespoons canola, olive, or sunflower oil

MAKES ¼ CUP · A basic for all salads and crudités, making this French dressing is much easier than dressing French! Just follow *la règle d'or*—the golden rule: one part vinegar to three parts oil. It's also important to always make it in the same order so you get the best emulsion. Vinegar first. Oil second. *Voilà!*

1. In the same bowl in which you will toss the salad, combine the vinegar with the salt and pepper, and stir using a wooden spoon. (Note: Salt doesn't dissolve in oil so it must be added before the oil.)

2. Add the first tablespoon of oil, stirring continuously, slowly adding the rest of the oil until the dressing is perfectly combined.

3. You can then either add the ingredients for the salad or store in an airtight container. It doesn't need to be refrigerated and can be kept for weeks.

Le Petit Truc To change the flavor, you can also add fresh herbs (thyme, chives, chervil, parsley, oregano, cilantro, etc.) or minced shallots to the mix. Make sure you add them after the salt and pepper but before the oil. One tablespoon of Dijon mustard can also be added to the vinegar to make a thicker dressing.

PÂTE BRISÉE

PIE DOUGH

Prep time: 5 minutes

VEGETARIAN · UNDER 30 MINUTES · CLASSIC

2 cups flour

1 egg

½ cup (1 stick) butter, diced, at room temperature

⅛ cup water

1 teaspoon salt

MAKES 1 PIECRUST · Pâtisserie—French pastry—is all about the crust. This basic crust can be used for many recipes, from savory quiches to sweet pies. It's much healthier than a store-bought crust. I like how easy and good this one is to make—it's so effortless that I can actually make it with my eyes closed!

1. Pour the flour into a large bowl, and make a well in the center.

2. Add the egg to the bottom of the well.

3. Start mixing, then add the diced butter. (If you're in a hurry, you can always premelt the butter for 30 seconds in the microwave, but make sure it doesn't melt so much that it becomes liquid.)

4. While stirring, slowly add the water and the salt.

5. Once the dough starts to come together, press with your fists to make it into a large ball.

6. Cover with plastic wrap for 30 minutes before rolling out and cooking.

Le Petit Truc To roll it out, use 2 sheets of parchment paper. Place the dough on one sheet, then place the second sheet on top of the ball of dough. Roll your pin over the top parchment paper sheet: this will allow you to roll out a thinner crust.

PÂTE SABLÉE

CRUMBLY SWEET PIE DOUGH

Prep time: 10 minutes ⚜ *Cook time: 15 minutes*

VEGETARIAN • UNDER 30 MINUTES • CLASSIC

FOR SWEET PIES

1¼ cups (2½ sticks) butter, diced, at room temperature

1½ cups almond flour

¾ cup brown sugar

2 teaspoons salt

1 egg

1 egg yolk

2 cups all-purpose flour

ADDITIONAL INGREDIENTS FOR THE MEGA-SABLÉE

¾ cup (1½ sticks) butter, at room temperature

½ cup brown sugar

MAKES 4 PIES • Pâte Sablée is a crust used for sweet pies. It means "sandy" crust, because of the way it is made: crumbling together butter and flour makes the mixture look like sand. This recipe is a two-in-one crust. You can just make the first recipe and use it for a sweet tart (add fruits on top of it and cook them together), or you can make it even better by baking it (and adding more sugar and butter) before adding the filling. I call this second option a Pâte Mega-Sablée. It is inspired by the great French pastry chef Philippe Conticini, who invented the *pâte supra sablée.*

TO MAKE SWEET PIES

1. In a large bowl, work the butter until it is very soft, like a face cream (we call butter like this *beurre pommade*). Whisk together the almond flour, the brown sugar, and the salt. Then add the egg and the egg yolk.

2. Pour the all-purpose flour onto a flat surface, create a well at the center, and pour the mixture into it.

3. Use your hands to mix everything together.

4. Place the dough on a sheet of parchment paper, place another sheet of parchment paper on top, and roll until the dough is equally spread out.

5. Wrap in plastic wrap and place in the fridge for 2 hours. ➳

6. You can then divide in 4 and use this crust as is for a simple sweet pie (Tarte aux Pommes [page 190], for instance).

TO MAKE MEGA-SABLÉE

1. Preheat the oven to 325°F.

2. Bake the prepared Pâte Sablée dough for 15 minutes.

3. Crumble the baked crust into a large bowl.

4. Add the additional butter and brown sugar, using your hands to mix it together.

5. You can then roll the dough out between 2 sheets of parchment paper until equally spread out.

6. Bake for 13 minutes.

Le Petit Truc You can also use the Mega-Sablée on top of baked fruit for a great crumble.

CRÈME CHANTILLY

FRENCH WHIPPED CREAM

Prep time: 5 minutes

VEGETARIAN · GLUTEN FREE · UNDER 30 MINUTES · CLASSIC

2 cups whipping cream

⅔ cup powdered sugar

MAKES 2 CUPS · A perfect addition to almost any dessert, whipped cream is always called *crème chantilly* in France, where it has been made for centuries. It's also common to use the term "*crème fouettée*" when not adding sugar. I always keep whipping cream in the fridge in case I have to make a last-minute dessert. Although you will need to prepare it several hours before using it, French whipped cream takes no time to make and is much healthier and more fun than ready-to-use whipped cream from the store.

1. An hour ahead of time, put the bowl of the stand mixer in the fridge, or even better, in the freezer for 20 minutes.

2. Put the whipping cream in the bowl. Start whisking slowly for 20 seconds, then whisk rapidly. When the cream starts to get thick, pour in the powdered sugar. Keep whisking until the cream is fluffy.

3. Keep in the fridge for 2 hours before serving.

PÂTE À CRÊPES

CRÊPES BATTER

Prep time: 5 minutes ✣ *Cook time: 1 minute for each crêpe*

Origin: Normandy

VEGETARIAN · UNDER 30 MINUTES · CLASSIC

3 eggs

2 cups flour

2 ½ cups whole milk
(or 2 cups whole milk
and ½ cup beer)

1 tablespoon butter

1 teaspoon salt

MAKES A DOZEN CRÊPES · Not only do the French have a special day for eating crêpes (La Chandeleur—every year on February 2), they love to eat and share them all year long. For breakfasts, snacks, dessert, and late-night munchies, this basic recipe can be used to make savory or sweet crêpes. For an easier-to-flip crêpe, you can add beer to the batter.

1. In a large bowl, whisk the eggs and slowly add the flour.

2. Keep whisking as you pour the milk in little by little (also add the beer if desired).

3. Cover and let the batter rest for at least an hour.

4. Once you're ready to cook a crêpe, melt the butter. Add the melted butter and salt to the batter at the last minute, whisking well.

Le Petit Truc To cook a crêpe, heat a lightly oiled pan over medium-high heat, take a small ladleful of batter, and pour it in the center of the pan. Immediately swirl the pan so that the batter spreads all over. Cook until the rim of the crêpe detaches itself from the pan, then use a wooden spatula to flip it onto the other side, cooking for about 1 additional minute.

BOUILLON DE VOLAILLE

CHICKEN BROTH

Prep time: 15 minutes ✦ Cook time: 2 hours

DAIRY FREE · GLUTEN FREE · CLASSIC

1 chicken carcass or
various poultry leftovers

2 carrots, peeled
and cut into 2 chunks

1 leek, white part only

4 cloves

1 onion

½ cup white wine

1 bouquet garni (see page 13)

6 peppercorns

MAKES 4 CUPS · Long before bone broth was a healthy trend, bouillon, the French broth, was a cornerstone of French cuisine. A healthy way to use leftover poultry, you can drink it as is or use it to add flavor to plenty of great recipes.

1. Put the carcass in a large stockpot. Add the carrots and leek. Stick the cloves into the onion and add to the pot.

2. Add the white wine and slowly add cold water until everything is submerged. Add the bouquet garni and the peppercorns.

3. Bring to a boil over medium heat. Lower the heat and simmer for 2 hours. Do not cover.

4. Strain the broth. Let it cool in the refrigerator after skimming off the fat that has appeared on the surface.

Le Petit Truc You can store the broth in the freezer in an ice cube tray. Add an ice cube of broth to soups or boiling water when making pasta or rice for even more flavor.

SAUCE BÉCHAMEL

BÉCHAMEL SAUCE

Prep time: 1 minute ✦ *Cook time: 10 minutes*

VEGETARIAN · UNDER 30 MINUTES · CLASSIC

⅓ cup butter

½ cup flour

4 cups whole milk

1 teaspoon salt

1 teaspoon freshly
ground pepper

1 teaspoon
ground nutmeg

MAKES 3 CUPS · This warm sauce is one of the "mother sauces" of French cuisine—*les sauces mères*—the most important sauces in traditional French cooking. It is used in many recipes and is a great base for other sauces.

1. Melt the butter over medium heat in a saucepan. It should not get brown. Remove from the heat and pour in the flour, whisking immediately by hand until the butter and flour are well mixed. Put back on medium heat until the mixture thickens slightly.

2. Pour the milk into the pan and increase the heat to medium high. The sauce should always be on the verge of boiling, as you whisk continuously until thick.

3. Add the salt, pepper, and ground nutmeg. Serve or store immediately.

Le Petit Truc Using the same process, you can also make a *sauce blanche*—a white sauce—by substituting broth for the milk. A tiny bit healthier than the milk version, this sauce is perfect for the lactose intolerant!

PÂTE FEUILLETÉE

PUFF PASTRY

Prep Time: 20 minutes, with 2 hours to chill

VEGETARIAN, CLASSIC

3 ¼ cups flour

1 tablespoon salt

1⅛ cup cold water

4½ sticks of butter,
at room temperature

MAKES 4 PIE CRUSTS · Now a staple of Greek and Middle Eastern cuisines, puff pastry was originally developed in France during the Renaissance period. The main ingredient for Millefeuille and many other pastries is dough. It is easier to buy store-bought dough, but making your own tastes better and is more satisfying.

1. In a large bowl, vigorously mix the flour, salt, and water. Using the palm of your hands, flatten the dough (this particular part is called the détrempe) and cover it with plastic wrap. Put in the fridge for 2 hours.

2. Spread the butter over a parchment paper sheet, add another sheet on top, and roll over it until it is a ¼ inch square. Put the flour mixture over another parchment paper sheet, and use a knife to make a cross on top. Put another paper sheet on top. Roll it until it's a ⅛ inch square. Add the butter at the center. Fold each corner of the dough on the butter, as if it was an envelope.

3. Gently roll the squared envelope into a rectangle. Fold it in three, to create a square. Give a ¼ turn to the dough, and roll it into a rectangle again. Fold in three. Wrap in plastic and put in the fridge for 30 minutes.

4. After 30 minutes, roll the dough into a rectangle again, fold in three, turn, roll and fold again. Wrap in plastic and put in the fridge for 30 minutes, and then repeat another time the rolling and folding.

5. You can use it at once or freeze it. Never shape it into a ball.

APÉRITIFS

CHAPTER THREE

"**T**U PASSES PRENDRE L'APÉRITIF?" ("Do you want to come over for an apéritif?") is very often the first invitation you get to a French house. *L'apéritif*—or *apéro*, for short—is something like a cult in France. It used to just refer to the drinks you would have quickly before lunch or dinner. But it now includes food as well, and it is a large part of the art of French dining. It takes only a short trip to the huge *apéritifs* aisle in a French supermarket to discover how the French are now obsessed with it.

Apéro can be served before the actual meal, and it can include a glass of wine, or a *pastis*, a traditional French alcohol. It is something like happy hour: a drink and some charcuterie, for example, while you meet your friends on a nice Parisian terrace. But it is also more and more a meal in itself, or as my mom calls it "*apéritif dinatoire*"—a lot of small plates of cheese and charcuterie over drinks, which actually could make a whole dinner and that allows for a more laid-back social occasion.

Now open that bottle of Bourgogne and repeat after me the two essential words of French *apéro*: "*santé*" or "*chinchin*"—cheers—while you clink each other's glasses!

TAPENADE NOIRE

BLACK OLIVE SPREAD

Prep time: 10 minutes

Origin: Provence

DAIRY FREE · GLUTEN FREE · UNDER 30 MINUTES · CLASSIC

1 cup pitted black olives, strained and dried

6 anchovy fillets, strained and dried

2 tablespoons capers, strained and dried

1 garlic clove, peeled and halved with the green germ removed

2 tablespoons olive oil

SERVES 8 · This is the perfect item for an *apéritif* in Provence! This delicious olive spread was invented in the southeast of France, where olives and olive trees are everywhere. Spread some tapenade on a thin slice of bread, open a bottle of chilled rosé, and you will almost feel like you are in Marseilles or Avignon.

1. Put the olives, anchovies, capers, and garlic into a food processor. Process until combined and add the olive oil. Keep processing until the mixture becomes a coarse paste.

2. Pour into a bowl and serve with sliced bread or as a dip.

Le Petit Truc You can replace 1 tablespoon of the olive oil with 1 tablespoon of cognac.

Pairing: Pair with chilled rosé.

RILLETTES

PORK SPREAD

Prep time: 15 minutes ✦ *Cook time: 7 hours* ✦ *Refrigeration time: 24 hours*

Origin: Loire Valley

DAIRY FREE · GLUTEN FREE · CLASSIC

---

3 pounds pork belly with the rind cut off and set aside

4 pounds pork shoulder with the rind cut off and set aside

4 tablespoons salt

2 tablespoons freshly ground pepper

2 tablespoons thyme

3 bay leaves

SERVES 8 · It's not Pâté (page 41 and 42); it's even better. This pork spread is perfect on a slice of bread. Add cornichons and a glass of red wine, and you're in charcuterie heaven! The secret? Seven hours of slow cooking.

1. Cut the pork belly in ½-inch strips. Chop the pork shoulders into 1-inch chunks.

2. Place a large French oven or cast-iron pot over medium heat. Brown the pork belly in it. Add the chunks of pork shoulder, brown on all sides, and cook for about 15 minutes.

3. Add cold water to cover the meat, cover, and cook on medium heat for 1 hour, stirring often.

4. Add salt, pepper, bay leaves, thyme, and the rinds. Reduce the heat to the lowest level, and simmer for 6 hours.

5. Take the rind and any bones out, discard, and turn off the heat. Let the pot cool at room temperature. When cold enough, the fat should float to the surface. Spoon out the fat and put in a separate bowl. Pour the meat into ceramic pots or glass jars. Wrap them and put in the fridge for 24 hours.

Le Petit Truc You can keep Rillettes in the refrigerator for a week.

Pairing: Pair with red wine.

PÂTÉ DE CAMPAGNE

COUNTRY PÂTÉ

Prep time: 10 minutes ✤ Cook time: 90 minutes ✤ Refrigeration time: 24 hours

DAIRY FREE · GLUTEN FREE · CLASSIC

½ pound pork belly

¼ pound beef or chicken liver

1 shallot, minced

1 tablespoon salt

1 tablespoon freshly ground pepper

1 tablespoon Espelette pepper or paprika

3 pounds sausage meat (breakfast sausage, for example)

4 sprigs of fresh thyme, divided

1 tablespoon minced fresh parsley

3 fresh bay leaves

SERVES 8 · This countryside pâté is a classic and a favorite of my grandmother, who finally gave me the recipe after a very long battle. You eat it cold with bread and cornichons. It's also perfect as an appetizer or a late-night snack!

1. Chop the pork belly and the liver into small pieces. Put in a food processor and process for 1 minute. Add the shallot, salt, pepper, and Espelette pepper. Process for another minute.

2. In a large bowl, combine the sausage meat with the pork belly and liver mixture. Add the leaves of 2 sprigs of thyme and parsley. Mix everything together.

3. Pour into a meatloaf pan. Add the bay leaves and remaining 2 thyme sprigs on top of the meat. Cover with plastic wrap and leave in the refrigerator for at least 24 hours.

4. The next day, preheat the oven to 360°F. Pour a 1-inch layer of cold water into a large baking pan and place the meatloaf pan in it. Cook for 90 minutes.

5. Serve cold, freeze, or store for up to a week in the refrigerator.

Pairing: Pair with a simple red wine, such as pinot noir.

PÂTÉ EN CROUTE

CRUST PÂTÉ

Prep time: 20 minutes ✤ Cook time: 45 minutes

CLASSIC

5 eggs, divided

½ pound ground veal

1 pound sausage meat

1 sprig of thyme

2 tablespoons minced fresh parsley

1 tablespoon Espelette pepper

1 tablespoon salt

1 teaspoon freshly ground pepper

½ cup crème fraîche or whipping cream

2 puff pastry sheets

1 egg yolk

SERVES 8 · Baked in a crust, Pâte en Croute is the fanciest and most delicious version of pâté. It is a delicacy and is even the subject of a worldwide competition each year in Paris. But that doesn't make it a difficult recipe to follow. The following recipe is more specifically for Easter, as you add hardboiled eggs. It is then called a Pâté de Pâques.

1. Preheat the oven to 400°F.

2. Boil 3 eggs for 8 to 9 minutes, then peel.

3. In a large bowl, mix the veal, sausage meat, thyme, parsley, Espelette pepper, salt, and pepper. In another bowl, whisk the other 2 eggs and add the cream. Add the egg mixture to the meat mixture and mix together.

4. In a meatloaf pan, lay down a puff pastry sheet. Pour half of the meat mixture in it. Then place the peeled, boiled eggs on the meat mixture, spaced 2 inches apart. Pour the rest of the meat over the eggs.

5. Cover with the second puff pastry sheet, pinch the edges so everything is glued together, and brush with egg yolk. Make a small hole in the middle with a knife. Use a piece of rolled parchment paper to create a small "chimney" so the steam can come out.

6. Bake for 15 minutes at 400°F, then for 30 minutes at 350°F.

Pairing: Pair with red wine or rosé champagne.

FEUILLETÉS À LA SAUCISSE

SAUSAGE IN PUFF PASTRY

Prep time: 15 minutes ✦ *Cook time: 18 minutes* ✦ *Refrigeration time: 30 minutes*

CLASSIC

4 breakfast sausages

3 tablespoons Dijon mustard

1 puff pastry sheet

1 egg yolk, whipped

MAKES ABOUT 30 FEUILLETÉS (8 SERVINGS) · Puff pastry is used in savory recipes, too, and great in these classic rolled sausages.

1. Use a fork to prick the sausages, then cook them in a hot nonstick pan over medium to high heat for 7 minutes (no oil needed). Let the sausages cool in the fridge.

2. Spread mustard over the puff pastry sheet.

3. Cut the sheet in 4 equal pieces. They should each be the width of a sausage.

4. Roll each sausage in a piece of mustard-covered puff pastry, sealing it with some drops of whipped egg yolk. Put in the fridge for 15 minutes.

5. Preheat the oven to 400°F.

6. Cut each rolled sausage into 1-inch slices and place them on a sheet of parchment paper. Using a pastry brush, cover them with egg yolk.

7. Bake for 15 to 18 minutes.

Le Petit Truc You can use different types of sausage—spicy kielbasa, for example—or, if you're lucky enough to find them at your grocery store in the United States, *boudin noir* or *boudin blanc*.

Pairing: Pair with a bubbly rosé, or with a *kir royale*—2 tablespoons of black-currant liqueur mixed into a cup of champagne.

GOUGÈRES

CHEESE PUFFS

Prep time: 15 minutes ✤ *Cook time: 25 minutes*

Origin: Burgundy

VEGETARIAN · CLASSIC

1 cup water

1 teaspoon salt

4 tablespoons butter, diced, at room temperature

1 cup flour

3 large eggs, beaten

2 ½ ounces Gruyère or aged Cheddar cheese, cut into ½-inch cubes

SERVES 6 · Coming from the same part of France that brought us Escargots (page 52), Boeuf Bourguignon (page 90), and Burgundy wine, Gougères are delicious, airy cheese puffs that make a great hors d'oeuvre at *apéritif*.

1. Preheat the oven to 400°F.

2. In a medium saucepan, add the water, salt, and butter. Bring to a boil over high heat, stirring well.

3. Once boiling, add the flour. Reduce the heat to low. Whisk with a wooden spatula for about 2 minutes, or until the mixture becomes smooth.

4. Let cool for a minute away from the heat, then pour in the beaten eggs. Keep whisking.

5. Add the cheese cubes and whisk until the cheese melts (about 2 minutes).

6. Using a tablespoon, make small balls of dough and place them on a sheet of parchment paper placed on a sheet pan.

7. Bake for 25 minutes or until the Gougères are golden. Serve immediately.

Le Petit Truc Add a tablespoon of Espelette pepper for a tasty twist.

Pairing: Pair with champagne.

CAKE SALÉ

SAVORY CAKE

Prep time: 10 minutes ✦ *Cook time: 45 minutes*

CLASSIC

3 eggs

1¼ cups of flour

2 teaspoons baking powder

1 teaspoon salt

1 teaspoon freshly
ground pepper

½ cup olive oil

½ cup whole milk

1 tablespoon butter

3 slices of ham, sliced in
½-inch matchstick-size pieces

½ cup pitted olives
(green or black)

1¼ cups grated cheese
(Comté, Gruyère,
or aged Cheddar)

SERVES 6 · A slice of savory cake is always very nice to share over a glass of wine with friends. I remember making this recipe a lot when I was a student, because it was so easy and delicious.

1. Preheat the oven to 350°F.

2. In a large bowl, whisk the eggs. Add the flour, baking powder, salt, and pepper. Slowly add the oil while whisking the mixture.

3. In a small saucepan, heat the milk over low heat, stopping before it reaches a boil. Add to the egg mixture and whisk.

4. Coat the inside of a loaf pan with butter. Place the ham, olives, and grated cheese into the bottom of the pan. Then pour the batter on top.

5. Bake for 45 minutes.

Le Petit Truc You know the cake is ready to take out of the oven when a knife plunged into it comes out clean. Always slice it after it has cooled down. You can also experiment with other combinations like smoked salmon and chives, bleu cheese and bacon, and so on.

FLAMMEKUECHE

THIN-CRUST BACON AND CREAM PIE

Prep time: 15 minutes ⁂ Cook time: 10 minutes

Origin: Alsace

UNDER 30 MINUTES · CLASSIC

2 cups flour

¼ cup canola oil,
plus 1 tablespoon

1 tablespoon salt,
plus 1 teaspoon

⅓ cup water

⅔ cup crème fraîche
or whipping cream

⅓ cup ricotta cheese, drained

1 teaspoon freshly
ground pepper

1 teaspoon ground nutmeg

3 onions, minced very thin

3 ounces bacon, cut into
matchstick-size pieces

SERVES 4 · This thin-crust bacon and cream pie should be eaten straight out of the oven, with your bare hands (and maybe a glass of Gewürztraminer, the traditional Alsatian white wine).

1. Pour the flour in a large bowl. Make a well in the center. Add ¼ cup of oil, 1 tablespoon of salt, and ⅓ cup of water. Knead until you can roll out easily. Cover with a damp cloth for an hour.

2. In another bowl, combine the crème fraîche, cheese, pepper, remaining teaspoon of the salt, and nutmeg. Stir well and add the tablespoon of canola oil.

3. Preheat the oven to 500°F.

4. Roll out the dough on a piece of parchment paper as thinly as possible. The flammekueche can be round or square but is always thin-crusted.

5. Spread the crème fraîche and cheese mixture over the dough with a spatula, leaving about ½ inch of uncoated dough on the edges.

6. Sprinkle the onions and the bacon evenly across the dough.

7. Put the pie on a sheet pan or a pizza stone. Bake for 8 to 10 minutes.

Le Petit Truc Prepare everything and make the pies when your guests arrive so you can share them straight out of the oven.

Pairing: Pair with an Alsatian white wine.

		28,00
		36,00
		36,00
		30,00
		36,00

...20" Gascogne moelleux	4,50	24,00
... Gaillac ... / Rouge	4,50	24,00
... Po... blanc	5,00	30,00
...he ...ron		30,00
...v... Lnguedoc	5,50	33,00
...ain... u	6,00	36,00
... Pennautier Cabardes		38,00

...SACE
...not blanc Klipfel	4,50	24,00
...not Gris Klipfel	5,50	33,00
...sling Klipfel	4,50	24,00
...wurztraminer Klipfel	5,50	33,00
...wurztraminer Laugel	Magnum	62,00

...IRE
...ncerre blanc / Rouge	8,00	42,00
...illy Fumé	8,00	42,00

...URGOGNE
...ardonnay H. Vezelay	5,00	30,00
...ablis Premier Cru	7,00	40,00
...con Rouge	6,00	35,00
...nay 1er Cru		50,00
...vrey Chambertin ...		

CORSE
Clos Poggiale

BORDEAUX
Cht Haut Du Groux Moe
Cht Ferrande Grave blanc
Cht Malbec Rouge
Cht L'Alouette Lalande Pom
Cht La Colombière St Emilio
Cht Barreyes Haut Médoc
Mademoiselle L. Haut Médoc
Josephine De Boyd Margaux
Cht Les Gravillons St Emilion

Cht Beau-Site St Estephe

ITALIE
Prosecco Le Viane De Alice
Pinot Grigio ____ blanc
Pinot Grigio Mirabello Rosé
Bardolino Cesarie
Nero D'Avola Adesso
Sollione Negroamaro Salento
Sollione Primitivo Salento
Amarone Classico Cesari

ESPAGNE
Rioja Crianza Anares

VIN DU MONDE
Kumala Chenin / Chardonn
(Afrique du Sud)
L'Avenir Pinotage
(Afrique du Sud)

APPETIZERS

CHAPTER FOUR

READING A FRENCH MENU can always seem a little bit confusing for an American tourist in Paris, or even at any French restaurant: In the French language, an *entrée* is not the main course; it is the course you start or enter the meal with. This is the same word that refers to entering a building . . . *une entrée*.

These appetizers are very important in the French culinary culture. The French don't want to eat a lot, but they do want to eat a lot of different things, and in small portions. I realized later in my life why my mother was so obsessed with us always having *une entrée* before we ate anything else. She was always making crudités—raw vegetables in salads (Carottes Rapées [page 55] or Concombre à la Crème [page 59], for example)—which was a great way for us to have some vegetables at the beginning of the meal and sate the hunger you first feel when sitting at the table. Basically, it's having a healthy and satisfying course first, and then meat, cheese, and sweets. Which is why you should never start with dessert first!

Some appetizers here are richer than others and are dedicated to dinner parties. They are a great way to start the meal on a nice note, and to have, as the French say, "*une mise en bouche*"—a foretaste of what is to come next.

SOUFFLÉ AU FROMAGE

CHEESE SOUFFLÉ

Prep time: 15 minutes ✢ *Cook time: 30 minutes*

Origin: Burgundy

CLASSIC

2 cups whole milk

½ cup (1 stick) plus
1 tablespoon butter, divided

1 cup flour

1 teaspoon ground nutmeg

1 teaspoon salt

1 teaspoon freshly
ground pepper

6 eggs, whites and yolks
separated

1½ cups cheese (Gruyère,
Cheddar, or Comté)

SERVES 6 · The best dish to impress! This cheese soufflé is to be served straight out of the oven, when it has just risen and is full of air and glamour. Be sure to put it in the oven exactly 30 minutes before serving, and do not open the oven while baking.

1. Preheat the oven to 375°F. In a small saucepan, bring the milk to a boil over medium heat.

2. In a large saucepan, melt ½ cup of butter over medium heat. Add the flour. Start whisking. Add the nutmeg, salt, and pepper. Slowly pour the warm milk over the butter and flour mixture, whisking until smooth and thick. Cool for 2 minutes.

3. Add 2 egg yolks. Keep whisking as you add the cheese. Then add 2 more yolks. Whisk until smooth, then add the last 2 yolks.

4. In the bowl of a stand mixer, whisk the egg whites until very firm. Add them tablespoon by tablespoon to the egg and cheese mixture, coating the egg whites.

5. Pour the mixture into a buttered 8-inch dish (preferably ceramic). Cook for 30 minutes, or until the top browns slightly.

Pairing: Pair with a dry white wine. A Loire Valley wine like Montlouissur-Loire would be your best bet (and not just because my grandmother and father live close by).

ESCARGOTS

SNAILS IN PARSLEY BUTTER

Prep time: 20 minutes ✦ *Cook time: 8 minutes* ✦ *Refrigeration time: 20 minutes*

Origin: Burgundy

GLUTEN FREE · UNDER 30 MINUTES · CLASSIC

1 shallot, minced

2 garlic cloves

3 tablespoons finely chopped fresh parsley

1 teaspoon salt

1 teaspoon freshly ground pepper

½ cup (1 stick) butter, at room temperature

24 snails (generally sold in cans of 12, so 2 cans), with shells

24 escargots shells

½ cup white wine

SERVES 4 · *Escargots de Bourgogne* is the French appetizer par excellence. *Oui,* we eat snails—and yes, they are delicious! Mostly because in this very French recipe they are cooked in butter, garlic, and parsley. My favorite part of the dish: dipping a piece of bread in the leftover sauce.

1. In the bowl of a food processor, combine the shallot, garlic, parsley, salt, pepper, and butter. Process for 1 minute, until smooth. Wrap and store in the fridge for 20 minutes.

2. Preheat the oven to 450°F.

3. Wash the snails. Pat them dry. Spoon out a full teaspoon of the flavored butter and place inside a snail shell. Place a snail inside the shell, then cover with 1 teaspoon of flavored butter, making sure the shell is totally full. Repeat for each snail shell.

4. Place the snails in the shells on a baking pan. Pour the white wine around the bottom of the pan. Bake for 8 minutes.

5. Serve immediately in the pan with plenty of fresh bread to dip in the sauce.

Le Petit Truc If you can't find shells, you can also just cook the snails topped with the flavored butter.

Pairing: Pair with a local white wine, Bourgogne Aligoté, or a bottle of dry white wine.

CÉLERI RÉMOULADE

CELERIAC SALAD IN RÉMOULADE SAUCE

Prep time: 10 minutes ✛ Refrigeration time: 1 hour

VEGETARIAN · CLASSIC

2 pounds celeriac

Juice of half a lemon

1 tablespoon Mayonnaise
(page 25)

1 tablespoon crème fraîche
or whipping cream

3 tablespoons minced
fresh parsley or tarragon

1 tablespoon capers, drained

3 cornichons, drained and
minced

SERVES 4 · Raw celeriac in a rémoulade sauce is a very common first course in France. One of the first sauces taught at cooking school, rémoulade was invented in France. But it is never spicy, and it is always white—contrary to the hot red sauce made in Louisiana where it was brought and adapted by the first French settlers.

1. Wash the celeriac, peel it, and grate it. Place the grated celeriac in a large salad bowl. Pour the lemon juice on the celeriac so it won't change color.

2. In a separate bowl, mix the Mayonnaise and the crème fraîche. Add the herbs, capers, and cornichons. Stir well. You just made a rémoulade sauce!

3. Add the rémoulade slowly to the celeriac, mixing well.

4. Leave in the fridge for at least 1 hour before serving.

Le Petit Truc To serve top with fresh parsley or a few leaves of a celeriac branch.

CAROTTES RÂPÉES

GRATED CARROTS

Prep time: 10 minutes ✦ *Refrigeration time: 3 hours*

VEGAN · VEGETARIAN · DAIRY FREE · GLUTEN FREE · CLASSIC

8 carrots, peeled with ends trimmed and leaves removed

Juice of 1 lemon

1 teaspoon salt

1 teaspoon freshly ground pepper

2 tablespoons olive oil

2 tablespoons finely chopped fresh parsley

SERVES 4 · The easiest French *entrée* and surely one of the healthiest, Carottes Râpées is a hit among French kids who are used to seeing them on the menu in the school cafeteria. Always try to make it a day ahead.

1. Grate the carrots with a box grater (using the largest holes) or a mandolin slicer.

2. In a large bowl, combine the lemon juice, salt, and pepper. Add the olive oil and whisk until well combined.

3. Add the parsley. Stir well, then add the grated carrots and toss for about 2 minutes.

4. Cover in plastic wrap and leave in the fridge for at least 3 hours.

Le Petit Truc You can make a sweeter version by adding 1 teaspoon of honey to the dressing and ½ cup of raisins to the carrots. Carottes Râpées are great with a tablespoon of ground cumin added to the dressing.

ASPERGES BLANCHES À LA SAUCE LAURENCE

WHITE ASPARAGUS

Prep time: 15 minutes ✛ *Cook time: 20 minutes*

Origin: Loire Valley

VEGETARIAN · GLUTEN FREE

FOR THE ASPARAGUS

2 pounds white asparagus, peeled

FOR THE SAUCE LAURENCE

½ cup crème fraîche or whipping cream

1 teaspoon salt

1 teaspoon freshly ground pepper

1 tablespoon green onions, finely chopped

1 tablespoon red wine vinegar

½ cup Vinaigrette (page 26)

SERVES 4 · You know it's springtime in France when white asparagus finally appear on the stands of the *primeurs*—the grocery stores that sell only fruits and vegetables. Besides being full of flavor, these gorgeous white vegetables are also low in calories. They are usually served with Vinaigrette (page 26). In my family, we also serve them with a white sauce we call *"sauce Laurence"* because it was my grandmother Laurence's specialty.

TO MAKE THE ASPARAGUS

1. Peel the asparagus carefully, as remaining skin can result in unwanted threads. Trim the asparagus about 1 inch from the bottom.

2. Fill a very large saucepan with water and bring to a boil. Plunge the asparagus into the boiling water. Cook for 20 minutes.

3. With a slotted spoon, remove the asparagus from the water, pat dry, and place on a large serving plate.

4. You can either eat the asparagus with a fork and knife, or savor them "family style" by grabbing the asparagus like a stick and dipping it in the sauce of your choice. ➤➤

TO MAKE THE SAUCE LAURENCE

In a medium bowl, mix the crème fraîche, pepper, salt, green onions, and red wine vinegar until well combined. Pour into a serving bowl and place on the table alongside a small bowl of Vinaigrette.

Le Petit Truc Sauce Laurence is a great dip for raw vegetables.

Pairing: Pair with a bottle of white wine from the Loire Valley or a sauvignon blanc.

CONCOMBRE À LA CRÈME

CUCUMBERS IN CRÈME FRAÎCHE

Prep time: 25 minutes ❖ Refrigeration time: 3 hours

VEGETARIAN · GLUTEN FREE

1 teaspoon salt, divided

2 cucumbers, peeled and cut into thin slices

¼ cup crème fraîche or whipping cream

1 tablespoon red wine vinegar

2 tablespoons finely chopped green onions

1 teaspoon freshly ground pepper

SERVES 4 · A great fixture on every *plateau de crudités*—the plate of raw vegetables often served as an appetizer along with Carottes Rapées (page 55) or Céleri Rémoulade (page 54)—Concombre à la Crème is a perfect, refreshing appetizer.

1. Sprinkle half of the salt on the cucumbers, and let them sit for 15 minutes.

2. Meanwhile, mix the crème fraîche, vinegar, green onions, pepper, and the rest of the salt in a large bowl.

3. Add the cucumber slices and stir well. Cover with plastic wrap and cool in the refrigerator for at least 3 hours.

Le Petit Truc My grandmother, Laurence, told me that the cream and vinegar mixture can also be used as a great dip for carrots or celery, for instance. Sometimes I substitute fresh mint for the green onions.

BETTERAVES EN SALADE

BAKED BEET SALAD

Prep time: 10 minutes ✦ Cook time: 2 hours

VEGAN · VEGETARIAN · DAIRY FREE · GLUTEN FREE

2 pounds beets, cleaned, dried, and wrapped in a paper towel and then wrapped in aluminum foil

1 tablespoon red wine vinegar

1 teaspoon salt

1 teaspoon freshly ground pepper

3 tablespoons canola oil or olive oil

1 tablespoon finely chopped fresh parsley

SERVES 4 · Sweet, full of color, low in calories, and so healthy! Beets are perfect to start a meal. I like to prepare them very simply like my grandmothers and mother used to, with a red wine vinegar dressing and parsley.

1. Preheat the oven to 350°F.

2. Put the wrapped beets in a baking dish or on a sheet pan and cook for 2 hours.

3. In a large bowl, mix the vinegar with the salt and pepper. Slowly add the oil until well combined.

4. Peel the baked beets by rubbing them with a paper towel until the skin comes off. Chop the beets into ½-inch cubes and add them to the bowl.

5. Add the parsley and toss well.

Le Petit Truc You can also add cubes of goat or feta cheese and walnuts to the mix.

HARENGS POMMES À L'HUILE

HERRING AND POTATO SALAD

Prep time: 10 minutes ✢ *Cook time: 20 minutes*

Origin: Paris

DAIRY FREE · GLUTEN FREE · UNDER 30 MINUTES · CLASSIC

2 pounds fingerling
potatoes

2 teaspoons salt, divided

1 teaspoon freshly
ground pepper

2 tablespoons white
wine vinegar

6 tablespoons canola oil

1 tablespoon finely chopped
green onions

1 sweet onion, minced

¼ cup white wine

8 smoked herring fillets
in oil, drained

SERVES 4 · Marinated herring and potato salad is on the menu of any good Parisian bistro. I love the fact that this potato salad is served lukewarm with the perfume of the white wine still steaming out of the potatoes.

1. Boil the potatoes (with their skin) in a large saucepan filled with cold water and a teaspoon of salt. Boil for 20 minutes.

2. Meanwhile, combine the remaining salt, pepper, and vinegar in a salad bowl. While whisking, add the oil one tablespoon at a time, green onions, and sweet onion.

3. Peel the boiled potatoes immediately and add them to the bowl. Toss well and pour the white wine on the potatoes.

4. Serve the potato salad with 2 herring fillets per person.

Pairing: Pair with a bottle of dry white wine, such as a Muscadet.

SALADS

CHAPTER FIVE

SALADS ARE THE PERFECT APPETIZER, or a great main course in themselves. They are a wonderful way to enjoy vegetables at their freshest, and are often a good way to discover locally grown produce as you travel through France . The basic idea of the salad is that it combines what you found and bought at the farmers' market with a nice Vinaigrette (page 26).

Les salades composées—combined salads—as they are often called, make a great lunch, and can easily be packed in a lunchbox, although some need to be eaten on the spot, as they combine cold and warm ingredients.

One big rule for all of them: the dressing makes all the difference, and it has to be homemade. As you discovered in chapter 2, it only takes a few seconds to prepare a vinaigrette from scratch, and the taste is so much better. I always try to make the dressing first, in the bowl where the salad ingredients will be tossed and served: it is a way to use less vinaigrette and, therefore, add fewer calories. Try to always toss the ingredients very well: the French say *"on la fatigue"*—tossing it so much that it looks tired but is also perfectly and delicately coated in oil and vinegar.

SALADE D'ENDIVES ET DE ROQUEFORT

ENDIVE AND BLEU CHEESE SALAD

Prep time: 10 minutes

VEGETARIAN · GLUTEN FREE · UNDER 30 MINUTES

6 endives

Juice of 1 lemon, divided

2 apples, peeled

½ pound bleu cheese
(preferably Roquefort or
Fourme d'Ambert)

1 tablespoon red wine vinegar

1 tablespoon Dijon mustard

1 teaspoon salt

1 teaspoon freshly
ground pepper

4 tablespoons canola oil

½ cup walnuts

SERVES 4 · Endives are common in France, and to my pleasure they are easy to find now that I live in the United States. They belong to the chicory family (like frisée or radicchio) and have a sweet and mildly bitter taste. This recipe is the perfect way to discover endives and to enjoy a salad during the winter while only using in season ingredients.

1. Wash the endives under cold water, and trim their feet off. Cut into ½-inch slices. Pour half the lemon juice on them.

2. Cut the apples in ½-inch cubes. Sprinkle remaining lemon juice on them and reserve. Cut the bleu cheese in ½-inch cubes.

3. In a large salad bowl, prepare the dressing by mixing the red wine vinegar with the Dijon mustard, salt, and pepper. Then add the canola oil little by little, whisking constantly until the dressing is thick and smooth.

4. Add the endives and toss well. Add the apples and toss until well coated. Then add the cheese and walnuts, and toss until well combined.

Pairing: Pair with a sweet white wine, such as Sauternes.

SALADE LANDAISE

DUCK CONFIT AND DUCK BACON SALAD

Prep time: 15 minutes ✦ *Cook time: 5 minutes*

Origin: Southwest of France

DAIRY FREE · GLUTEN FREE · UNDER 30 MINUTES

1 head romaine lettuce

1 medium shallot, diced

1 tablespoon red wine vinegar

1 tablespoon salt

1 teaspoon freshly ground pepper

10 cherry tomatoes, halved

8 duck confit gizzards

½ pound smoked duck bacon, thinly sliced

¼ cup pine nuts

SERVES 4 · This salad uses typical ingredients from Les Landes, a beautiful region in southwestern France: a land of pine trees, duck farms, and party-loving people who know how to live and eat well. I love the fact that this recipe mixes warm ingredients with cold ones. To enjoy even more, add a slice of another local specialty, foie gras.

1. Wash and drain the lettuce and tear it into bite-size pieces.

2. In a salad bowl, whisk the shallot, red wine vinegar, salt, and pepper, until well combined.

3. Add the halved cherry tomatoes followed by the lettuce, and toss until coated. Reserve.

4. Heat a large nonstick skillet over high heat, and sauté the gizzards for 3 to 5 minutes, until they lose their blue color and turn slightly red. Then pour the warm gizzards and the rendered fat over the salad. Toss well. Add the smoked duck bacon and the pine nuts, toss again, and serve immediately.

Pairing: Pair with a full-bodied red wine, such as a cabernet sauvignon.

SALADE LYONNAISE

BACON, POACHED EGG, AND FRISÉE SALAD

Prep time: 10 minutes ✣ Cook time: 15 minutes

Origin: Lyon

DAIRY FREE · GLUTEN FREE · UNDER 30 MINUTES · CLASSIC

½ pound bacon, cut into
½-inch strips

1 medium shallot, peeled
and diced

2 tablespoons red wine
vinegar, divided

4 eggs

1 bunch of frisée or
head of romaine

1 teaspoon salt

1 teaspoon freshly
ground pepper

SERVES 4 · This salad comes from Lyon, also known as the capital of French gastronomy because so many great chefs started there. I went to college in Lyon and learned how to make this dish there. It will always be one of my all-time favorites. Among other things, I love that you use the warm rendered fat of the bacon to make the dressing.

1. Heat a nonstick skillet over medium heat. Add the bacon, let it sweat for a minute and add the diced shallot. Using a wooden spoon, stir well for about 3 minutes, or until the mixture becomes translucent.

2. Fill a medium saucepan with water and add 1 tablespoon of red wine vinegar. Break each egg into a ramekin. When the water begins to boil, lower the heat until the water simmers gently, and then softly drop each egg into the water. When the egg whites begin to congeal, use a spoon to shape them into a ball and cook for 2 more minutes. Use a slotted spoon to remove the eggs from the pan and place them in ice water or serve immediately.

3. Put the frisée into a large salad bowl and pour the bacon and the caramelized shallot onto it, along with the warm bacon fat in the skillet. Toss the salad, add the salt and pepper, and toss again.

4. Top the salad with the poached eggs and serve.

SALADE NIÇOISE

Prep time: 15 minutes ⟡ *Cook time: 10 minutes*

Origin: Provence

DAIRY FREE · GLUTEN FREE · UNDER 30 MINUTES · CLASSIC

3 large eggs

1 garlic clove, peeled

1 tablespoon red wine vinegar

1 teaspoon salt

1 teaspoon freshly
ground pepper

3 tablespoons olive oil

2 cups arugula

3 medium tomatoes,
thinly sliced

4 green onions, finely sliced

8 anchovy fillets in oil,
drained

1 (5-ounce) can tuna in oil

6 large basil leaves, shredded

½ cup unpitted Niçoise olives

SERVES 4 · Invented in the city of Nice on the Mediterranean Coast, this salad is a symbol of the French Riviera. It is best when made with the freshest ingredients straight from the farmers' market, never-boiled potatoes, or French beans. Niçois people are so serious about their salad that they give an award every year to the most faithful recipe!

1. Place the eggs in a small saucepan, cover with water, and boil for 10 minutes. Using a slotted spoon, take the eggs out and plunge into a bowl of water. Reserve.

2. Rub the garlic clove on the inside of a large salad bowl. Add the vinegar, salt, and pepper. Whisk and add the olive oil tablespoon by tablespoon until well combined.

3. Add the arugula, tomatoes, and green onion, tossing to coat.

4. Add the anchovies and tuna, and toss again.

5. Peel and quarter the eggs. Place over the salad with the basil and black olives.

Le Petit Truc Both legendary chefs Auguste Escoffier and Julia Child mistakenly added boiled potatoes to the recipe, to the horror of natives from Nice. If you choose to do so, just don't invite your Niçois friends!

Pairing: Pair with a rosé.

SALADE DE PISSENLITS

DANDELION SALAD

Prep time: 10 minutes ✦ Cook time: 5 minutes

DAIRY FREE · GLUTEN FREE · UNDER 30 MINUTES · CLASSIC

½ pound bacon, cut into ½-inch strips

2 medium shallots, peeled and diced

1 tablespoon red wine vinegar

4 eggs

½ pound fresh young dandelion leaves

1 teaspoon salt

1 teaspoon freshly ground pepper

SERVES 4 · You know it's springtime in France when the Salades de Pissenlits start appearing on restaurant menus. I was always bewildered by the idea of eating *pissenlits* because as a kid we would pick them in the fields nearby. Dandelions are not only very good, they are also great for your health.

1. Heat a nonstick skillet over medium heat. Add the bacon, let it sweat for a minute, then add the diced shallots. Using a wooden spoon, stir well for about 3 minutes, or until the mixture becomes translucent.

2. Fill a medium saucepan with water and add 1 tablespoon of red wine vinegar. Break each egg into a ramekin. When the water begins to boil, lower the heat until the water simmers gently, and then softly drop each egg into the water. When the egg whites begin to congeal, use a spoon to shape them into a ball and cook for 2 more minutes. Use a slotted spoon to remove the eggs from the pan and place them in ice water or serve immediately.

3. Put the dandelions in a large salad bowl, then pour the bacon and the caramelized shallots over the leaves, along with the warm bacon fat in the skillet. Toss the salad, add the salt and pepper, and toss again.

4. Top the salad with the poached eggs and serve.

Le Petit Truc Make sure you use young dandelion leaves: the more they age, the more bitter they become.

SALADE DE RIZ

RICE SALAD

Prep time: 10 minutes ✦ *Cook time: 20 minutes* ✦ *Refrigeration time: 1 hour*

DAIRY FREE · GLUTEN FREE

1 tablespoon salt,
plus 1 teaspoon

1 cup uncooked rice

Juice of 1 lemon

1 teaspoon freshly
ground pepper

3 tablespoons olive oil

1 medium red bell pepper,
seeded and chopped into
½-inch squares

2 medium tomatoes,
cut into thin slices

1 (5-ounce) can tuna
in water, drained

12 anchovy fillets in oil,
drained

¼ cup black olives, pitted

SERVES 4 · This rice salad is great for a picnic or a day at the beach. You can make it ahead and don't need to store it in a cooler. Two of my friends have a never-ending fight over what is the best recipe. I hope this one settles them down!

1. Fill a large saucepan with water, and bring to a boil. Add a tablespoon of salt, and throw in the rice. Cook for 18 minutes. Drain and reserve.

2. Squeeze the lemon juice into a large salad bowl. Combine with remaining teaspoon of salt and pepper. Slowly add the olive oil and whisk until the dressing is thick.

3. Add the rice, diced bell pepper, tomato slices, tuna, anchovy fillets, and black olives. Toss well.

4. Cover with plastic wrap and cool in the fridge for 1 hour before serving.

Pairing: Serve with a chilled bottle of rosé.

SALADE PARISIENNE

PARISIAN SALAD

Prep time: 15 minutes ✤ *Cook time: 10 minutes*

Origin: Paris

GLUTEN FREE · UNDER 30 MINUTES · CLASSIC

4 eggs, boiled, peeled, and halved

1 serving of Vinaigrette (page 26)

1 teaspoon Dijon mustard

1 head romaine lettuce, leaves torn into bite-size pieces

½ cup fresh button mushrooms, thinly sliced

3 thick slices of ham, cut into ½-inch squares

½ cup Gruyère cheese, cut into ½-inch cubes

½ cup finely chopped fresh parsley

SERVES 4 · This salad reminds me of having lunch in Paris at the *bistrot du coin*—corner bistro. Salade Parisienne is what is called a *salade complète*, a salad that serves as your whole lunch and gives you enough energy for a day in a crazy-busy city like Paris.

1. Fill a medium saucepan with water, and boil the eggs for 10 minutes. Put the boiled eggs in ice water, let them cool down, and peel them. Halve them.

2. In a large salad bowl, combine Vinaigrette and Dijon mustard.

3. Add the romaine, stir well, then add the mushrooms, ham, and cheese. Add the parsley.

4. Place the hardboiled eggs on top of the salad and serve.

Le Petit Truc You can make croutons by cutting slices of stale bread in ½-inch cubes, rubbing them with a garlic clove, and frying them for 5 minutes in 1 tablespoon of butter.

SALADE DE LENTILLES VERTES

GREEN LENTIL SALAD

Prep time: 15 minutes ✦ *Cook time: 25 minutes*

Origin: Auvergne

DAIRY FREE · GLUTEN FREE · CLASSIC

1 cup lentilles du Puy—
French green lentils

¼ pound bacon, cut into
½-inch strips

2 shallots, peeled and minced

1 carrot, peeled and cut
into ½-inch slices

½ cup white wine

2½ cups cold water

1 teaspoon salt

1 teaspoon freshly
ground pepper

1 bay leaf

1 tablespoon thyme

1 teaspoon Dijon mustard

1 tablespoon red wine vinegar

4 tablespoons olive oil

SERVES 4 · Some call it *"le caviar vegetal"*—vegetarian caviar—and I couldn't agree more. I love French lentils, the green kind that are grown in Le Puy in the center of France. They are full of antioxidants and folic acid, which is great for pregnant women. This salad is another favorite of mine in the winter.

1. Rinse the lentils well and drain.

2. Heat a large, preferably nonstick saucepan and brown the bacon for 1 minute over high heat. Once the bacon begins to sweat, add the shallots, stir well, and cook for 2 minutes. Then add the carrot slices and green lentils, and stir well over high heat for 1 minute. Pour the white wine and the water into the pan, stir, and bring to a boil.

3. Once boiling, add the salt, pepper, bay leaf, and thyme. Reduce heat to low, cover, and simmer for at least 20 minutes. Once the water has completely evaporated, remove from heat and let cool.

4. In a salad bowl, mix the mustard and red wine vinegar. Add the olive oil, whisking well. Pour the lentil mixture into the salad bowl, toss until well coated, cover, and place in the fridge. Serve cold.

Le Petit Truc You can make this recipe with leftover lentils from a Petit Salé aux Lentilles (page 98). Just add Vinaigrette (page 26).

OMELETTES, EGGS, AND QUICHES

CHAPTER SIX

LES OEUFS—EGGS—ARE ESSENTIAL to the French diet. Because you somehow always have some in the fridge, they always make the best last-minute lunch. Add an egg to any of the salads in chapter 5 if it is not there already, and you have another perfect dish!

When in Paris, I love to have a simple Omelette aux Fines Herbes (page 77) at lunch, with a nice *salade verte*—green lettuce and Vinaigrette (page 26). It's always a quick and light *déjeuner* on the menu of almost any French bistro (sometimes served with French fries, too—not so low in calories). And the Oeufs Cocotte (page 79), eggs cooked in cream in ramekins, are just heaven on a cold winter day (and so quick to make!).

Eggs are not a breakfast item in the French culture, where *petit déjeuner* is mostly for sweet things: bread, jam, or croissants. They are rather eaten for lunch, just like my beloved quiches. Starting with the iconic Quiche Lorraine (page 82), savory tarts and pies are great for *déjeuner,* too, and are my own favorite to take to work or on a picnic! They are also great to serve at *apéritif,* cut into small slices.

OMELETTE AUX FINES HERBES

HERB OMELETTE

Prep time: 5 minutes ✦ *Cook time: 5 minutes*

VEGETARIAN · GLUTEN FREE · UNDER 30 MINUTES · CLASSIC

6 eggs

2 tablespoons finely chopped green onions

1 teaspoon salt

1 teaspoon freshly ground pepper

1 tablespoon finely chopped fresh parsley

1 tablespoon butter

SERVES 2 · Just fresh eggs, fresh herbs, and a hot pan. This simple equation yields a dish famous all over the world. I like my omelette "naked" with fresh parsley and green onions. Along with a simple salad with Vinaigrette (page 26), it's the light easy lunch par excellence.

1. In a large bowl, mix the eggs with the green onions, salt, pepper, and parsley with a fork or a whisk for about 2 minutes.

2. In a nonstick frying pan, melt the butter over medium heat. Once the butter spreads evenly in the pan, pour in the egg mixture. Stir immediately with a wooden spatula, especially around the edges of the pan.

3. When the bottom of the omelette is golden and the top is still a little bit runny, tilt the pan over a serving plate. Using a wooden spatula, gently unstick the omelette from the pan and let it fold on itself onto the plate.

4. Serve immediately.

Pairing: Pair with a white wine or even a glass of champagne.

OMELETTE JAMBON FROMAGE

HAM AND CHEESE OMELETTE

Prep time: 10 minutes ✦ Cook time: 5 minutes

GLUTEN FREE · UNDER 30 MINUTES

2 slices of jambon blanc
or thinly sliced cooked ham

6 eggs

1 teaspoon salt

1 teaspoon freshly
ground pepper

⅓ cup grated Gruyère,
Comté, Emmental, or
Cheddar cheese

1 tablespoon butter

1 tablespoon finely chopped
fresh parsley

SERVES 2 · You can add almost anything to an omelette, once you have the right amount of eggs, and the technique to roll it perfectly. This recipe is one of the most classical there is, with ham and cheese. You can also try it with tomatoes, avocados, escargots, or spicy sausage.

1. Cut the ham into ½-inch squares.

2. In a large bowl, whisk the eggs with the salt and pepper. Add the cheese and the ham, and whisk again for 2 minutes.

3. Heat a nonstick frying pan over medium heat. Melt the butter: it should sizzle, not get brown. Make sure that the butter spreads evenly in the pan and then pour in the egg mixture. With a wooden spatula, start to stir immediately, especially around the edges of the pan.

4. When the bottom of the omelette is golden and the top is still a little bit runny, tilt the pan over a serving plate. Using the wooden spatula, gently unstick the omelette from the pan and let it fold on itself onto the plate.

5. Sprinkle the parsley on top and serve immediately.

OEUFS COCOTTE

EGGS IN RAMEKINS

Prep time: 10 minutes ✦ *Cook time: 15 minutes*

VEGETARIAN · GLUTEN FREE · UNDER 30 MINUTES · CLASSIC

1 tablespoon butter

1 teaspoon salt

1 teaspoon freshly
ground pepper

⅔ cup crème fraîche
or whipping cream

4 eggs

3 tablespoons finely chopped
fresh chives

SERVES 4 · One of my favorite egg recipes: it's easy, it's cheap, and of course, it's mouthwatering! Oeufs Cocotte is a typical family dish in which you basically bake an egg in a ramekin, usually with cream. I love that every guest gets their own ramekin! Plus, the options are unlimited—you can add tomatoes, cheese, smoked salmon, or even caviar.

1. Preheat the oven to 400°F.

2. Rub butter inside 4 small ramekins, and sprinkle salt and pepper on top.

3. In a small saucepan, heat the cream over medium heat and stir. The cream should not reach the boiling point.

4. Pour 2 tablespoons of warm cream in each ramekin and break an egg on top, leaving the yolk intact.

5. Prepare a *bain-marie*—hot-water bath—by pouring a 1-inch layer of water into a larger baking dish and placing the ramekins in it. Put the baking dish in the oven and bake for 10 minutes. Watch closely: the egg whites should not become opaque, and the yolk should still be runny.

6. Sprinkle about 1 tablespoon of fresh chives over each egg.

7. Serve directly in the ceramic ramekins with toasted bread for dipping.

OEUFS MIMOSA

DEVILED EGGS

Prep time: 15 minutes ✦ *Cook time: 20 minutes*

VEGETARIAN · DAIRY FREE · GLUTEN FREE

8 eggs

½ cup Mayonnaise
(page 25)

2 tablespoons finely chopped
green onions, divided

1 teaspoon salt

1 teaspoon freshly
ground pepper

SERVES 6 · These hardboiled eggs served with Mayonnaise (page 25) are a trip down memory lane. This is the kind of recipe my grandmothers—and even their mothers—would make. Yellow like mimosa flowers and a great appetizer, this dish makes a nice hors d'oeuvre.

1. Fill a large saucepan with water, bring to a boil, and place the eggs in it. Boil for 10 minutes. Prepare a bowl of ice water and submerge the eggs in it, then remove, peel, and halve each egg.

2. Using a tablespoon, scoop out the egg yolks and set them aside in a small bowl. Mash the yolks with a fork. In another small bowl, mix ⅔ of the mashed yolks with the Mayonnaise. Mix in 1 tablespoon of the green onions and the salt and pepper.

3. Using a teaspoon, fill each egg white with the mayonnaise and egg yolk mixture.

4. Sprinkle the leftover egg yolks and green onions onto the eggs. Serve cold.

Le Petit Truc You can make this recipe even easier by scooping a teaspoon of mayonnaise onto a boiled egg that has been halved. This variation is called *oeufs mayonnaise* and is a classic on Parisian bistro menus.

QUICHE COURGETTES MENTHE

ZUCCHINI-AND-MINT GOAT CHEESE QUICHE

Cook time: 40 minutes

VEGETARIAN

1 Pâte Brisée (page 27)

1 tablespoon olive oil

3 large zucchini, thinly sliced

3 eggs

½ cup crème fraîche
or whipping cream

½ cup whole milk

12 mint leaves, finely chopped

1 teaspoon salt

1 teaspoon freshly
ground pepper

½ cup fresh goat cheese or
feta, crumbled

SERVES 4 · This zucchini and mint quiche is a regular guest at home. I love making it a night ahead to bring to work the next day, which gives the mint more time to imbue the dish with its subtle perfume. It's also great for buffets or picnics.

1. Preheat the oven to 350°F.

2. Place the dough on a sheet of parchment paper, place another sheet on top of the dough, and roll it out to a 13-inch round. Take a 12-inch pie plate, remove the top sheet of parchment paper, and place the dough and the bottom sheet of parchment paper on the pie plate. Fold the dough overhang under, and crimp the edge. Cut away the parchment paper that is extending out of the plate.

3. In a nonstick skillet over medium heat, heat the oil, add the zucchini, and fry for 5 minutes.

4. In a large bowl, whisk the eggs and cream. Add the milk, mint, salt, and pepper and stir until smooth.

5. Place the zucchini in the bottom of the pie. Crumble the cheese over the zucchini and pour the custard on top.

6. Bake for 40 minutes.

Le Petit Truc Serve lukewarm with a green lettuce salad and Vinaigrette (page 26) or cold the following day.

QUICHE LORRAINE

Prep time: 15 minutes ✦ Cook time: 40 minutes

Origin: East of France

CLASSIC

1 Pâte Brisée (page 27)

3 large eggs

½ cup crème fraîche
or whipping cream

½ cup whole milk

½ teaspoon salt

1 teaspoon freshly
ground pepper

1 teaspoon ground nutmeg

4 ounces bacon, cut into
½-inch strips

SERVES 4 · There would be no quiche without the iconic Quiche Lorraine, the first ever invented and by far the best. My friend Deborah, who is from eastern France, says that whenever you have people coming over to your place for the first time, you should always make a *quiche de bienvenue*—a welcome quiche!

1. Preheat the oven to 350°F.

2. Place the dough on a sheet of parchment paper, place another sheet on top of the dough, and roll it out to a 13-inch round. Take a 12-inch pie plate, remove the top sheet of parchment paper, and place the dough and the bottom sheet of parchment paper in the pie plate. Fold dough overhang under, and crimp the edge. Cut away the parchment paper that is extending out of the plate. Then, with a fork, make small holes all over the dough. Set aside.

3. Whisk the eggs in a small bowl. Gradually add the cream and milk. Keep whisking as you add the salt, pepper, and nutmeg.

4. Place bacon all over the crust, and pour in the custard.

5. Bake for 40 minutes.

Le Petit Truc I like spreading Dijon mustard onto the crust before adding the bacon for more moisture. You can also add ½ cup of your favorite grated cheese, but it won't be an authentic Lorraine anymore.

Pairing: Pair with a blond beer or a white wine, such as a sauvignon blanc.

TARTE À LA MOUTARDE ET À LA TOMATE

DIJON MUSTARD AND TOMATO TART

Prep time: 10 minutes ✦ Cook time: 30 minutes

VEGETARIAN · CLASSIC

5 medium-size tomatoes

1 tablespoon salt

1 Pâte Brisée (page 27)

3 tablespoons Dijon mustard

1 teaspoon freshly
ground pepper

1 tablespoon thyme
or rosemary

SERVES 4 · This savory pie is every French family's companion in the summer, when you want an easy and good dish to share and enjoy (get the glass of rosé ready!). Dijon mustard and tomatoes definitely make a great couple.

1. Preheat the oven to 350°F.

2. Cut the tomatoes in thin slices, sprinkle salt on them and reserve.

3. Place the dough on a sheet of parchment paper, place another sheet on top of the dough, and roll the dough out to a 13-inch round. Take a 12-inch pie plate, remove the top sheet of parchment paper, and place the dough and the bottom sheet of parchment paper on the pie plate. Fold the dough overhang under, and crimp the edge. Cut away the parchment paper that is extending out of the plate.

4. Spread the Dijon mustard evenly on the pie dough. Lay the tomato slices one by one on the mustard, starting at the edge of the dish. Once you've finished the first round, go on layering tomato slices until you reach the middle ("snail like"). Sprinkle pepper and thyme on top.

5. Bake for 30 minutes and serve immediately.

Le Petit Truc Sprinkle ½ cup of grated Gruyère or Cheddar cheese on top.

Pairing: Pair with a rosé from Provence.

PISSALADIÈRE

ONION, ANCHOVY, AND OLIVE PROVENÇAL PIZZA

Prep time: 15 minutes · Cook time: 65 minutes

Origin: Provence

DAIRY FREE · CLASSIC

⅓ cup olive oil

4 pounds onion, minced

1 garlic clove

1 bay leaf

2 tablespoons rosemary
or thyme

¼ teaspoon salt

2 tablespoons freshly ground
pepper, divided

1 (13.8-ounce) ready-made
pizza dough

18 anchovy fillets,
drained

SERVES 4 · Long before pizza, there was Pissaladiere! This dish is always a pleasure to make and share with friends, especially if you can eat it outside, on a warm summer night.

1. Heat the oil in a large saucepan on medium heat. Add the minced onions, garlic clove, bay leaf, rosemary, salt, and pepper. Lower the heat, cover, and simmer for 45 minutes.

2. Meanwhile, roll out your dough on a sheet of parchment paper, and until it is a 10-by-15-inch rectangle. Cover the dough with a damp cloth, and let it rise for about 1 hour, or until it doubles in height.

3. Turn the heat under the saucepan off when almost all the oil is gone and the onions are golden. Remove the garlic and the bay leaf.

4. Preheat the oven to 500°F.

5. Roll out the dough again on a sheet of parchment paper, until it's ⅛ inch thick. The Pissaladière is always a rectangle, and it should be the size of your sheet pan. Spread the onions on the dough. Place the anchovy fillets on it, within the rectangles. Place an olive at the center of each rectangle.

6. Bake for 20 minutes. Season with remaining pepper immediately after removing from the oven.

Le Petit Truc Serve immediately with Salade Niçoise (page 68).

Pairing: Pair with a rosé from Provence.

PLATS DU JOUR

CHAPTER SEVEN

ANOTHER FRENCH PHRASE that made its way all around the world is "*plat du jour*"—the dish of the day. Every bistro promotes its special of the day, usually a heartwarming, traditional meal. Or as some American people might call it, "comfort food." These are dishes you can drive all the way across town to have, or invite all your friends over to share together. The following recipes come from all around the country, but all have the same common feature: they are meant to be shared with people you love!

Most of the dishes featured here also have one thing in common that I think is crucial to what makes French cuisine great: they are *plats à mijoter*, dishes that simmer for a long time. They are my favorite! They only take a very small amount of time to prepare—all you need is a good French oven, or any good quality cast-iron pot, put everything in it (if possible in the right order), place a lid on it, simmer over low heat, and . . . wait for the magic to happen! Or, as my chef uncle, Bernard, always says: let time make it better!

CASSOULET

Prep time: 10 minutes (prepare overnight) ✦ *Cook time: 4 hours*

Origin: Southwest of France

DAIRY FREE · GLUTEN FREE · CLASSIC

2 pounds dried white beans (preferably Tarbais, otherwise cannellini)

6 confit duck or goose legs

1 sweet onion, minced

½ pound diced tomatoes

4 garlic cloves, peeled, divided

3 Toulouse or kielbasa sausages, cut into 1-inch slices

½ pound pork belly

1 bouquet garni (see page 13)

1 shallot, peeled

1 teaspoon salt

1 teaspoon freshly ground pepper

SERVES 6 · This traditional dish from southern France is hard to adapt totally in the United States because it's made of local French ingredients not always easy to find. I adapted some for your convenience. Anyway, it's always *un régal*—a treat!

1. The day before, soak the white beans in cold water.

2. Pour the drained beans into a large pan filled with water, place over medium heat, and boil for 30 minutes. Pour into a colander to drain.

3. Render the fat of the duck legs in a frying pan over medium heat, then place the legs on a separate plate. To the same pan, add the onion, and cook for 1 minute. Add the tomatoes and 3 cloves of minced garlic and cook for 5 minutes.

4. In another pan, fry the sausages over medium heat for 5 minutes.

5. Rub a clove of garlic on the inside of a large ceramic plate or a large cast-iron pot. Place the pork belly at the bottom of the dish, then add the beans, tomato mixture, bouquet garni, shallot, salt, and pepper. Bring to a boil over high heat. Once boiling, reduce the heat, cover with water, and simmer for 90 minutes.

6. Add the duck and the sausage, and cover with water. Simmer for an hour. A crust will form on the top of the dish—break the crust and add some water to cover. Simmer on very low heat for 1 more hour.

Pairing: Pair with a young red wine (one that hasn't aged too much), like Beaujolais.

BOEUF BOURGUIGNON

BEEF BURGUNDY

Prep time: 15 minutes ✢ *Cook time: 3 hours and 15 minutes*

Origin: Burgundy

DAIRY FREE · GLUTEN FREE · CLASSIC

4 ounces thick bacon, cut into ½-inch strips

1 large onion, minced

4 medium carrots, cut into ½-inch slices

2 pounds chuck steak, cut into 1-inch cubes

1 bottle red wine (preferably cabernet sauvignon)

1 bouquet garni (see page 13)

1 teaspoon salt

1 teaspoon freshly ground pepper

1 pound button mushrooms, chopped

SERVES 6 · My go-to *plat à mijoter,* since I was a student. Originally from Burgundy, where good wine and good meat abounds, this slow-cooked beef and red wine stew is one of the most traditional and easy French recipes! You can serve it with boiled potatoes or fresh pasta.

1. Place a large French oven, or a large pot with a thick bottom, over medium heat. Brown the bacon for a couple of minutes, then add the minced onion and sauté for 5 minutes. Add the carrots. Cook for 2 minutes, then add the beef, and brown on each side.

2. Add the bottle of red wine, bouquet garni, salt, and pepper, and bring to a boil over medium heat.

3. Once boiling, cover and turn the heat to low. Simmer for 3 hours.

4. Thirty minutes before serving, add the mushrooms, and let them simmer with the rest of the sauce.

Le Petit Truc Cuts of beef are not the same in France and in the United States, and it took me years to get it right. My rule is: always use stew meat. I sometimes use banana heel, a part of the feet I had never heard of before. You can also use beef cheeks or oxtail. Mixing different parts of the animal is even better!

DAUBE PROVENÇALE

BEEF, TOMATO, AND OLIVE STEW

Prep time: 15 minutes ✦ Cook time: 3 hours and 15 minutes

Origin: Provence

DAIRY FREE · GLUTEN FREE · CLASSIC

1 tablespoon olive oil

1 onion, minced

2 pounds beef shanks or cheeks, cut into 1-inch cubes

2 carrots, peeled and cut into ½-inch slices

1 bottle white wine

3 tablespoons tomato paste

2 garlic cloves, peeled and minced

Peel of half an orange

1 bouquet garni (see page 13)

1 teaspoon salt

1 teaspoon freshly ground pepper

½ cup pitted black olives

SERVES 4 · Olives, tomatoes, and thyme, the three essential ingredients of Provençal cuisine, make this slow-cooked beef recipe the Boeuf Bourguignon of the south of France. Serve warm with *pâtes fraîches*—fresh pasta—or polenta and a nice glass of rosé from Provence.

1. In a large French oven or pot, warm the oil over medium-high heat. Add the onion. Stir and cook slowly for 3 minutes. Add the beef, browning on each side for 5 minutes.

2. Add the carrots, stir well, and cook for 2 minutes. Then pour the bottle of wine into the pot.

3. Bring to a boil over high heat and add the tomato paste, garlic, orange peel, bouquet garni, salt, and pepper. Cover and reduce the heat to low. Simmer for 3 hours.

4. Thirty minutes before serving, add the black olives, cover again, and simmer until serving time.

Pairing: Pair with a Côtes de Provence rosé.

POT-AU-FEU

BEEF STEW WITH VEGETABLES

Prep time: 15 minutes ✣ *Cook time: 3 hours*

DAIRY FREE · GLUTEN FREE · CLASSIC

**3 pounds beef shank,
cut into 2-inch chunks;
or stew beef, cut into 1-inch
cubes; or a mix of both**

4 cloves

1 large onion

1 bouquet garni (see page 13)

1 tablespoon salt

**1 teaspoon freshly
ground pepper**

4 medium carrots, halved

4 leeks, green parts discarded

**2 medium turnips, trimmed
and quartered**

**1 pound bone marrow,
cut into 2-inch pieces**

6 medium potatoes

SERVES 6 · Pot-au-feu is one of the cornerstones of French cuisine. This slow-cooking stew with vegetables has been made for centuries. In the past, it was literally a pot on the fire that you would fill with whatever you found in the garden or at the market. Back in the nineteenth century, some restaurants were famous for never cleaning their pot and just adding meat and vegetables and water to it. Serve with a jar of cornichons and Dijon mustard on the table.

1. Fill a very large pot with cold water. Add meat. Bring to a boil over medium heat. Skim the fat off the surface. Cover and reduce the heat to low, simmering for 1 hour.

2. Stick the cloves into the onion. Add the onion, the bouquet garni, the salt, and the pepper. Cover and simmer for 1 more hour.

3. Add the carrots, leeks, and turnips. Simmer for at least 1 hour.

4. Thirty minutes before serving, add the bone marrow and potatoes.

5. For an appetizer, spoon out the broth into a large soup bowl and serve with toasted slices of bread. ➳

6. Using a slotted spoon, remove the vegetables, meat, and bone marrow. Serve on a separate plate.

Le Petit Truc If you make the Pot-au-feu a day in advance, you can store it in the fridge and skim off the solidified fat on top. By the way, this is the original "bone broth" recipe, with all its amazing benefits!

BLANQUETTE DE VEAU

VEAL STEW IN CREAM SAUCE

Prep time: 20 minutes ✤ Cook time: 2 hours

GLUTEN FREE · CLASSIC

FOR THE VEAL STEW

**3 pounds veal shoulder,
cut into 2-inch cubes**

4 cloves

1 onion

1 bouquet garni (see page 13)

1 teaspoon salt

**1 teaspoon freshly
ground pepper**

**3 carrots, cut into
½-inch pieces**

2 leeks, green part discarded

**1 celery stalk,
cut into ½-inch pieces**

2 tablespoons butter

1 pound button mushrooms

FOR THE CREAM SAUCE

4 egg yolks

Juice of 1 lemon

**¾ cup crème fraîche
or whipping cream**

SERVES 4 · Veal is hard to find in the United States, which is why I miss Blanquette de Veau so much. Whenever I can find good quality meat, I make this veal stew in cream sauce. Blanquette is a symbol of French *cuisine bourgeoise,* which developed in France in the nineteenth century. It's a typical winter dish, the kind you like to prepare for the whole family on Sunday. Serve with white rice.

TO MAKE THE VEAL STEW

1. Fill a large French oven or cooking pot with water. Add the veal. Bring to a simmer, cover, and keep on low heat for 1 hour. Skim the fat off the top.

2. Stick the cloves into the onion. Add the onion, bouquet garni, salt, and pepper. Bring slowly to a simmer again, cover, and cook for another 30 minutes. Add the carrots, leeks, and celery. Cover and simmer for another 30 minutes.

3. In a small saucepan, melt the butter over medium heat. Add the mushrooms, cover, and cook for 5 minutes. Set aside.

4. Ten minutes before serving, use a slotted spoon to take the meat and vegetables out of the pot. Place in a serving dish. Add the mushrooms. ➵

TO MAKE THE CREAM SAUCE

1. Whisk the egg yolks in a bowl and add the lemon juice, cream, and 1 ladleful of broth from the pot.

2. In a medium saucepan, bring 2 cups of the veal broth to a boil until it has reduced by half. Pour in the egg mixture, whisking constantly for 5 minutes or until the sauce thickens. Pour over the vegetables and the meat.

LA POTÉE AU CHOU

CABBAGE AND PORK STEW

Prep time: 15 minutes ✦ *Cook time: 3 hours*

Origin: Auvergne

DAIRY FREE · GLUTEN FREE · UNDER 30 MINUTES · CLASSIC

3 pounds pork shoulder,
cut into 1½-inch cubes

1 pound pork belly, ½-inch
thick, cut into 3-inch slices

1 bouquet garni (see page 13)

1 teaspoon salt

1 teaspoon freshly
ground pepper

4 cloves

1 onion

1 cabbage, cut into 6 chunks

4 carrots, cut into 3 chunks

6 kielbasa sausages
or any smoked sausages

10 medium-size potatoes,
washed

SERVES 6 · Cabbage and pork stew is a traditional recipe from Auvergne, a rural region in the center of France, where the mountains and the harsh climate are a perfect setting for this winter meal!

1. Fill a large pot with cold water.

2. Add the pork shoulder and pork belly. Bring to a boil over medium heat. Add the bouquet garni, salt, and pepper. Stick the cloves into the onion. Add to the saucepan. When the water starts boiling, lower the heat. Spoon the fat from the top of the pot. Cover and simmer for 1 hour.

3. Add the cabbage, carrots, and sausages, and cook for at least 1 more hour, preferably 2.

4. Thirty minutes before serving, add the potatoes to the pot and continue simmering.

5. When ready to serve, with a slotted spoon take out the potatoes and the vegetables, and place them in a large presenting dish. Take out the meat and place it on top. Each guest should help himself or herself to the vegetables and meat.

Le Petit Truc Serve with a pot of Dijon mustard on the table.

Pairing: Pair with a young red wine (one that hasn't aged too much), like Beaujolais.

PETIT SALÉ AUX LENTILLES

PORK SHOULDER AND GREEN LENTIL STEW

Prep time: 15 minutes ✷ Cook time: 2 hours and 15 minutes

Origin: Auvergne

GLUTEN FREE

1 tablespoon butter

8 ounces bacon, cut into ½-inch strips

2 onions

2 pounds pork shoulder, whole

2 carrots, thinly sliced

4 cups water

4 cloves

1 onion

1 bouquet garni (see page 13)

1 teaspoon salt

1 teaspoon freshly ground pepper

1 cup lentilles du Puy— French green beans

1 pot of Dijon mustard (for serving)

SERVES 4 · *Petit salé* is pork that has been brined in salt for 2 days to preserve it longer. It's almost impossible to find in the United States, but I adapted the recipe for you to enjoy this great pork and French lentil stew, a classic for winter.

1. In a large French oven or pot, melt the butter over medium heat. Add the bacon, and cook for 1 minute. Add the onions and cook for 5 minutes.

2. Add the pork shoulder, browning on each side for 5 minutes. Add the carrots and stir well. Pour in the water and bring to a boil over medium heat.

3. Stick the cloves into the onion. Add to the pot with the bouquet garni, salt, and pepper. Bring to a boil, cover, and reduce to low heat. Simmer for 1½ hours. Then add the lentils and stir well. Bring to a boil over medium heat, cover again, and reduce to low heat. Simmer for another 30 minutes.

4. Serve warm with a pot of Dijon mustard on the table.

Le Petit Truc You can add smoked sausage to the pot (Morteau sausage, ideally) 1 hour before serving.

CHOUCROUTE GARNIE

FRENCH DRESSED SAUERKRAUT

Prep time: 20 minutes ✦ *Cook time: 2 hours*

Origin: Alsace

DAIRY FREE · GLUTEN FREE · CLASSIC

1 tablespoon sunflower oil

1 pound pork belly, ½-inch thick, cut into 3-inch slices

1 large onion, minced thin

1 pound pork shoulder

2 pounds sauerkraut, rinsed and drained

2 cups white wine

8 juniper berries

1 teaspoon caraway seeds

4 peppercorns

4 garlic cloves, peeled and minced

1 teaspoon salt

1 teaspoon freshly ground pepper

8 small potatoes, peeled

4 frankfurter sausages

4 smoked Polish kielbasa sausages

SERVES 6 · Sauerkraut and choucroute are nearly the same dish—one is the German version and one is the French. This incredible dish celebrates the shared history of France and Germany. A specialty of Alsace, an eastern region of France that was part of Germany at some point, Choucroute Garnie is a wholesome dish that can be made lean by omitting the sausage.

1. Put a large pot over medium heat and heat the oil. Add the pork belly slices. Brown them on each side. Add the onion and cook for 5 minutes. Add the pork shoulder, and brown on each side. Add the sauerkraut, stir again, and add the white wine. Add the juniper berries, caraway seeds, peppercorns, garlic, salt, and pepper.

2. Cover the mixture with water and bring to a boil over medium heat. Cover and reduce to low heat. Simmer for 1½ hours.

3. Thirty minutes before serving, add the potatoes and the sausages to the pot, cover again, and continue cooking slowly.

Le Petit Truc Serve warm with a pot of Dijon mustard on the table.

Pairing: Pair with a good bottle of Gewürztraminer white wine.

GALETTE DE SARRASIN COMPLÈTE

BUCKWHEAT CRÊPES WITH CHEESE AND HAM

Prep time: 65 minutes (prepare overnight) ✦ *Cook time: 5 minutes*

Origin: Brittany, West of France

GLUTEN FREE · UNDER 30 MINUTES · CLASSIC

FOR THE BATTER (MAKES ENOUGH FOR 24 GALETTES)

8 cups buckwheat flour

6 cups water, divided

2 tablespoons fleur de sel

1 egg

FOR THE GALETTES COMPLÈTES

1 tablespoon butter

3 slices of ham, halved

6 eggs

¼ cup grated Gruyère, Comté, or Cheddar cheese

1 teaspoon salt

1 teaspoon freshly ground pepper

MAKES 6 GALETTES · Don't mention crêpes when traveling to Brittany! The Bretons only talk about galettes made out of buckwheat (gluten-free people, this will soon be your favorite recipe!), that they use to make savory, taco-like dishes, as well as sweet desserts (my favorite is the galette with salted butter and sugar, so simple and so good)! This recipe is for the traditional *galette complète* with ham and cheese.

TO MAKE THE BATTER

1. In a large bowl using a wooden spoon or even your own clean hands, mix the buckwheat flour with 4 cups of cold water and the fleur de sel. Break the egg into the bowl, mix again, then cover and refrigerate for, ideally, 12 hours.

2. The next day, add the 2 remaining cups of water, and whisk well. Let the batter rest for an hour at room temperature and use as the crêpes batter.

TO MAKE THE GALETTES COMPLÈTES

1. Place your crêpe pan or a nonstick frying pan over high heat. Melt the butter in it and pour in a ladleful of batter right before the butter becomes a light hazelnut brown color.

2. When bubbles start appearing all over, turn the galette, put half of a slice of ham in the middle, 2 tablespoons of grated cheese, and break an egg on top.

3. Fold the corners of the galette so as to create a square shape. Wait for the egg to cook completely and slide the galette out of the pan. Season with salt and pepper.

Le Petit Truc You can fill your galette with lox and cream cheese, cooked mushrooms and grated cheese, or anything you please.

Pairing: Pair with a hard cider.

TARTIFLETTE

CHEESE, BACON, AND POTATO CASSEROLE

Prep time: 15 minutes ✦ *Cook time: 45 minutes*

Origin: Savoie, the Alps

GLUTEN FREE · CLASSIC

2 pounds potatoes,
cut into 1½-inch cubes

½ pound bacon,
cut into ½-inch strips

1 sweet onion, minced

¼ cup white wine
(preferably Apremont, a
white wine from Savoie)

1 teaspoon ground nutmeg

1 Reblochon

1 teaspoon salt

1 teaspoon freshly
ground pepper

SERVES 6 · Tartiflette is the national winter dish of France. A local specialty of Savoie, the region of France that welcomed two winter Olympic games, and where thousands of people flock every winter to enjoy some of the best skiing on Earth, Tartiflette is also so easy you can make it without too much effort after a tiring day of skiing. All you need are potatoes, bacon, and Reblochon—a cheese from Savoie that has a delicious nutty taste. It can be bought at good cheesemongers in the United States, but you can substitute Délice du Jura or Raclette or Morbier (in the last case the recipe is called *Morbiflette*).

1. Fill a large pan with cold water and add the potatoes. Boil for 20 minutes, then drain the potatoes in a colander and set aside.

2. Preheat your oven to 400°F.

3. Heat a nonstick frying pan over medium heat, and brown the bacon for a minute. Add the onion, and cook for 5 minutes. Add the boiled potatoes, salt, pepper, and nutmeg, stir well, and cook for another 5 minutes on high heat.

4. Pour in the white wine, stir for a couple of minutes, and remove from the heat. Pour into a large gratin dish.

5. Slice the Reblochon into 2 and lay both halves over the potatoes with the rind up. The Reblochon should cover the whole dish. Never take the rind off! It's part of the beauty and deliciousness of the dish.

6. Bake for 25 minutes. Serve immediately.

Le Petit Truc Serve with a green lettuce salad in Vinaigrette (page 26).

Pairing: Pair with a bottle of sweet white wine.

SOUPS

CHAPTER EIGHT

IT'S OF COURSE A *classique* of French cuisine, so much so that for a long time, the French would call dinner *souper,* as in the meal when you have soup. Taking part in the *Souper du roi* (dining alongside Louis XIV, the Sun King, in Versailles) was the honor of a lifetime!

Paul Bocuse, the "pope of Nouvelle Cuisine," invented a soup for a state dinner that is to this day the most famous and upscale soup I have ever heard of: "*la soupe VGE*" (VGE, Valéry Giscard d'Estaing, was president of France back then). It is made with fresh black truffles and foie gras, and presented under a dramatic puff pastry dome. *Incroyable!*

But then, you don't have to be an amazing chef to be able to enjoy *la bonne soupe . . .*

In my family, as in many French families, soup was the dish of choice at dinner all winter (and cold, chilled soup like Soupe Vichyssoise [page 108] in the summer). And my great-grandfather would even have some in the morning, for breakfast!

Another French tradition I love is *faire chabrot.* After a nice bowl of soup, you pour some wine into the bottom of your plate and drink it, "to rinse it all." It used to be very traditional in some rural parts of France, and I would love to make it trendy again!

POTAGE BONNE FEMME

LEEK, POTATO, AND CARROT SOUP

Prep time: 10 minutes ✦ Cook time: 45 minutes

VEGETARIAN · GLUTEN FREE · CLASSIC

1 tablespoon butter

½ pound carrots, cut into
½-inch chunks

½ pound leeks, green parts
discarded, minced

1 pound potatoes, peeled and
cut into ½-inch cubes

6 cups water

1 bouquet garni (see page 13)

1 teaspoon salt

1 teaspoon freshly
ground pepper

SERVES 4 · Using traditional vegetables found during the winter, this recipe is easy, classic, and cheap. You don't even need a food processor or a food mill to make it! Potage Bonne Femme literally means "good woman soup."

1. In a large saucepan, melt the butter over medium heat until it sizzles without becoming brown. Add the carrots, leeks, and potatoes and stir well until they caramelize slightly.

2. Pour the water over the vegetables. Add the bouquet garni, salt, and pepper and bring to a boil. Reduce to low heat and simmer for 30 minutes. Remove the bouquet garni.

3. Serve immediately.

Le Petit Truc You can substitute broth for the water, and play with different peppers to change the flavor. I love using Neelamundi peppercorns from India. You can also add a tablespoon of crème fraîche or whipping cream just before serving.

Pairing: Pair with a full-bodied red wine, such as a cabernet sauvignon.

SOUPE VICHYSSOISE

VICHYSSOISE

Prep time: 10 minutes ✢ *Cook time: 40 minutes* ✢ *Refrigeration time: 90 minutes*

GLUTEN FREE · CLASSIC

1 tablespoon butter

1 onion, chopped

3 leeks, green part discarded, minced

2 potatoes, peeled and cubed

1 teaspoon salt

1 teaspoon freshly ground pepper

½ cup chicken stock

1 cup whole milk

⅓ cup crème fraîche or whipping cream

8 fresh parsley leaves

SERVES 4 · French people love a cold soup in the summer. Did you know that the most famous of them all, Vichyssoise, was invented in the United States? French chef Louis Diat created it in 1917 at the Ritz-Carlton in New York. It is now popular in France, too, where top French chefs compete to create the best recipe.

1. In a large saucepan, melt the butter over medium heat. Add the onion and cook slowly for 5 minutes, stirring often. Add the leeks and the potatoes, stir well, and cook for another 5 minutes. Add the salt, pepper, and chicken stock and bring to a boil.

2. Reduce to low heat. Pour in the milk, stir, and simmer for 30 minutes.

3. Pour into the bowl of a food processor and process until smooth. Pour the mixture into a serving bowl and let it cool at room temperature for about 30 minutes.

4. Add the cream, stir well, and leave the bowl in the fridge for 1 hour.

5. Decorate with parsley leaves and serve cold.

Le Petit Truc My favorite cold soup in the summer is even easier to make. My mom would serve us super cold whole milk in a bowl in which to dip *biscottes* (cooked toast) or day-old bread.

Pairing: Pair with a dry white wine.

SOUPE POIREAU POMMES DE TERRE

POTATO AND LEEK SOUP

Prep time: 10 minutes ✴ Cook time: 45 minutes

GLUTEN FREE · CLASSIC

1 tablespoon butter

3 leeks, green part discarded, finely chopped

1 pound potatoes, peeled and cubed

1 teaspoon salt

1 teaspoon freshly ground pepper

4 cups chicken stock

SERVES 4 · Potato and leek soup is the most basic and maybe most commonly eaten soup in France. This recipe is also the basis for what I call "Soupatou," the soup with everything. Using the same process, you add any vegetables you have in the refrigerator, cook, process, *et voilà!*

1. In a large saucepan, melt the butter over medium heat. Add the leeks, stir well, and brown slightly for 2 minutes. Add the potatoes, stir again, and cook for another 2 minutes. Add the salt and pepper and the stock, and stir well.

2. Bring to a boil over high heat, then reduce to low and simmer for 30 minutes.

3. Pour the soup into a blender or food processor (or use my favorite, the hand mixer), and process for 2 minutes. Serve warm.

Le Petit Truc Add a tablespoon of crème fraîche at the end for an even smoother result.

SOUPE À L'OIGNON

FRENCH ONION SOUP

Prep time: 15 minutes ✦ *Cook time: 20 minutes*

Origin: Paris

CLASSIC

4 tablespoons butter, divided

2 sweet onions, minced

1 tablespoon all-purpose flour

1 cup white wine

5 cups beef stock

1 teaspoon salt

1 teaspoon freshly ground pepper

4 large slices of bread, preferably a halved day-old baguette

½ cup grated cheese (Comté, Gruyère, or aged Cheddar)

SERVES 4 · It's almost dawn in Paris and you've been enjoying *les nuits parisiennes* so much that you still don't want to go to bed: Soupe à l'Oignon is the best remedy! I love this grated cheese onion soup that is said to have been invented by French King Louis XV. As the story goes, he was hungry in the middle of the night and could only find onions and bread.

1. Preheat the oven to 450°F.

2. Heat a large saucepan over medium heat, and melt 3 tablespoons of butter. Add the onions. Stir with a wooden spatula for about 5 minutes. When the onions are golden, sprinkle the flour over them and brown slightly. Pour in the white wine and beef stock. Add the salt and pepper, bring to a boil, cover, and reduce to medium heat for 10 minutes.

3. Spread the rest of the butter on the slices of bread. Toast them in the hot oven for 4 minutes, flipping them so each side browns slightly.

4. Pour the soup into an ovenproof soup bowl or casserole dish. Cover with the grilled toasts and sprinkle generously with grated cheese. Leave the dish in the oven for 10 minutes and remove before the grated cheese gets too brown.

5. Serve hot.

Pairing: Pair with a sweet white wine.

SOUPE AUX ORTIES

STINGING NETTLE SOUP

Prep time: 10 minutes ✦ *Cook time: 40 minutes*

Origin: Loire Valley

VEGETARIAN · GLUTEN FREE

1 pound fresh stinging nettles

1 tablespoon butter

1 pound potatoes, peeled and cubed

3 cups water or chicken broth or beef broth

1 teaspoon salt

1 teaspoon freshly ground pepper

4 tablespoon crème fraîche or Mexican crema

SERVES 4 · Yes, they sting, but not when cooked! You can sometimes find stinging nettle at farmers' markets or in specialized grocery stores, but it's even easier to get it on your own: I always find some in my backyard or in the forest. Just use a good pair of gloves! One of my favorite soups, Soupe aux Orties has a color so green the Grinch would be jealous.

1. Wearing gloves, remove the leaves from the top of the nettle stalks. Wash them thoroughly and let them dry.

2. In a large saucepan, melt the butter over medium heat. Add the stinging nettle leaves. Cook for 5 minutes, stirring constantly. Add the potatoes and stir for another 2 minutes. Pour in the water. Add the salt and pepper. Bring to a boil. Cover and cook for 30 minutes over low heat. Using a hand mixer or food processor, process for about 2 minutes or until smooth.

3. Serve on individual plates, adding a tablespoon of cream to each serving.

Le Petit Truc When I am lucky enough to find fresh stinging nettles, I always set some aside to freeze in resealable bags. You can add stinging nettles to any French soup, adding a bright green color and plenty of antioxidants.

Pairing: Pair with a young red wine, like a pinot noir.

GARBURE

WHITE BEAN, DUCK, AND PORK SOUP

Prep time: 15 minutes (prepare overnight) ✦ *Cook time: 3 hours and 15 minutes*

Origin: Southwest of France

DAIRY FREE · GLUTEN FREE · CLASSIC

½ pound dried white beans (preferably Tarbais, otherwise cannellini)

6 confit duck legs

1 large onion, finely chopped

3 leeks, green part discarded, cut into 1-inch chunks

½ pound of jambon de Bayonne, or smoked ham hock

3 turnips, halved

4 carrots, cut into 1-inch slices

2 celery stalks, sliced

1 bouquet garni (see page 13)

1 tablespoon Espelette pepper or paprika

½ teaspoon salt

1 teaspoon freshly ground pepper

1 cabbage, cut into big chunks

4 medium potatoes, peeled and cubed

SERVES 6 · It's, in a way, the Cassoulet (page 89) of soups. A very traditional dish in southwest France, Garbure is a complete and delicious dish that can feed a whole family and their friends for a few days. It's made of all the traditional ingredients from the region, including duck, ham, white beans, and Espelette pepper.

1. A day before, soak the white beans in cold water. Drain the next day.

2. In a very large pot over medium heat, brown the confit duck legs for 5 minutes, rendering a lot of fat. Take the legs out and place them on a separate plate. Add the onion and brown for 5 minutes. Then add the leeks and cook for 2 minutes. Fill the pot with cold water and bring to a boil.

3. Add the ham, turnips, carrots, celery, bouquet garni, Espelette pepper, salt, and pepper (the ham is already salty). Cover, reduce the heat to low, and simmer for at least 2 hours, periodically spooning out the fat.

4. Add the white beans and the cabbage. Cook for another hour.

5. Thirty minutes before serving, add the potatoes and the confit duck legs. Remove the bouquet garni before serving.

6. On each plate, first place the vegetables, then a piece of ham, then a piece of duck. Then pour broth over each serving.

Pairing: Pair with a full-bodied red wine, such as a cabernet sauvignon.

SOUPE DE POTIRON

PUMPKIN SOUP

Origin: Loire Valley

Prep time: 10 minutes ✦ *Cook time: 30 minutes*

VEGETARIAN · GLUTEN FREE

1 (2-pound) pumpkin

1 teaspoon salt

1 teaspoon freshly
ground pepper

3 cups whole milk

SERVES 4 · When fall came, my grandmother loved to use the pumpkin in the garden to make a delicious and sweet soup. This is her recipe.

1. Peel the pumpkin, spoon out the seeds and the fibers, discard, and cut the flesh into big chunks.

2. Fill a large saucepan with water, and bring to a boil over high heat. Add the pumpkin, salt, and pepper. Reduce to a medium heat, and cook for 20 minutes. Don't cover. When the pumpkin is soft, take it out of the water with a slotted spoon, place it on a plate, and reserve.

3. Empty the saucepan, add the cooked pumpkin chunks and the milk. Cook together for another 10 minutes over medium heat; the milk should never boil. Using a hand mixer or a food processor, process until smooth.

4. Serve warm.

Le Petit Truc To sweeten it even more, add a tablespoon of sugar. Some people also add a teaspoon of ground cinnamon.

Pairing: Pair with a young red wine (one that hasn't aged too much) from the Loire Valley, such as Gamay or pinot noir.

VELOUTÉ DE CHATAÎGNES

CHESTNUT SOUP

Prep time: 10 minutes · Cook time: 30 minutes

GLUTEN FREE

3 cups chicken broth

1 pound roasted chestnuts

1 bouquet garni (see page 13)

1 teaspoon salt

1 teaspoon freshly
ground pepper

⅔ cup crème fraîche
or whipping cream

SERVES 4 · Chestnut Soup is a great pleasure in winter. I always have cooked chestnuts and UHT (ultra-high-temperature) whipping cream in the pantry, to be able to make a great last-minute appetizer.

1. In a large saucepan, combine the broth, chestnuts, bouquet garni, salt, and pepper. Bring to a boil, then reduce the heat and simmer for 20 minutes.

2. Using a food processor or a hand mixer, process until smooth. Add the cream and process again.

3. Serve warm.

Le Petit Truc My father makes a great chestnut soup in which he adds button mushrooms. He still keeps his technique a secret, but here is how I make mine, which is almost as good. Cook ½ pound of diced button mushrooms in 1 tablespoon of butter, add the chestnuts and the broth, and proceed the same way!

SOUPE À L'OSEILLE

SORREL SOUP

Origin: Normandy

Prep time: 10 minutes ✦ *Cook time: 35 minutes*

GLUTEN FREE

1 tablespoon butter

1 shallot, minced

1 pound sorrel, chopped

1 pound potatoes, peeled and cubed

1 teaspoon salt

1 teaspoon freshly ground pepper

3 cups chicken stock or homemade chicken broth

1 cup whipping cream

SERVES 4 · Its tart and lemony taste has made sorrel a very traditional fresh herb to use in French cuisine. Sorrel soup is the best way to discover its amazing flavor. Should you not find sorrel, you can use the same process to make *soupe de cresson*—watercress soup.

1. In a large saucepan, melt the butter over medium heat. Add the shallot, stir well, reduce the heat to low, cover, and cook for 5 minutes, stirring occasionally. Add the sorrel, stir well, and cook for about 5 minutes.

2. Add the potatoes, salt, and pepper. Stir well and then add the chicken stock. Bring to a boil, reduce the heat to medium, and cook for 15 minutes.

3. Using a hand processor or a food processor, process until smooth.

4. Just before serving, add the whipping cream and stir well.

Pairing: Pair with a bottle of young red wine (one that hasn't aged too much) from the Loire Valley.

VELOUTÉ DE CHAMPIGNONS

CREAM OF MUSHROOM SOUP

Prep time: 10 minutes ✦ Cook time: 20 minutes

GLUTEN FREE · UNDER 30 MINUTES

2 tablespoons butter

1 medium shallot,
finely chopped

1 pound button mushrooms

2 cups chicken stock

1 cup water

1 teaspoon freshly
ground pepper

1 teaspoon salt

½ cup crème fraîche
or whipping cream

SERVES 4 · Smooth like velvet, *velouté* is a creamy soup that is always smooth and rich. This is a very popular soup and is usually a hit with kids.

1. In a large saucepan, melt the butter over medium heat. Add the diced shallot, stir well, and cook for about 5 minutes. Add the mushrooms and let them sweat for about 5 minutes. Stir well until the mushrooms soften.

2. Add the chicken stock and the water, and stir well. Add the salt and pepper.

3. Bring to a boil over high heat, then reduce heat to low, cover the saucepan, and simmer for 15 minutes.

4. Using a food processor or hand mixer, process for about 2 minutes or until smooth. Add the cream and whisk well. Simmer on very low heat until dinnertime.

Le Petit Truc To add a decorative twist, serve this *velouté* with a fresh parsley sprig over each bowl.

TARTINES

CHAPTER NINE

121
TARTINE FROMAGE DE CHEVRE JAMBON
Goat Cheese and Ham Tartine

122
TARTINE POIRE FOURME D'AMBERT
Pear and Bleu Cheese Tartine

123
TARTINE FOIE GRAS KAKI
Persimmon and Foie Gras Tartine

124
TARTINE FROMAGE BLANC RADIS
Radish and Fresh Cheese Tartine

126
CROQUE MONSIEUR BÉCHAMEL
Grilled Cheese and Ham Sandwich in Béchamel Sauce

127
CROQUE MONSIEUR MAISON
Baked Grilled Cheese and Ham Sandwich

128
PAIN PERDU
French Toast

129
PAIN PERDU SALÉ
Savory French Toast

YOU'RE IN A CAFÉ IN PARIS. Just ordered your *café crème*. *"C'est tout?"* Wonders the garçon, in a good mood. "Is that all?" Of course, you could be a total tourist, and ask for a croissant. But if you want to be a true *parisien*, you'll ask for a tartine. A slice of good bread, usually baguette, buttered with . . . butter. Great, colorful, flavorful butter. Maybe some jam, on the side (but trust me, you don't need it). Take it in one hand, firmly, dip it deep in the coffee, and bite generously. You just had a Parisian breakfast and discovered the joy of tartines.

A tartine is literally the piece of bread on which you spread things—*tartiner* in French. It used to be a snack that you would have for breakfast, or as a treat (like the other big French childhood classic: bread, butter, and a tablespoon of cocoa powder—so good), or with spreadable savory dishes like Pâté (pages 41 and 42) or Rillettes (page 40).

But now tartine has turned into a whole dish, which you can have as a main course, served with a green salad in Vinaigrette (page 26). The most sought after are made with *pain Poilane*, a sourdough bread made by Boulangerie Poilâne, that is made following very ancient techniques, and is still considered the crème de la crème of breads.

TARTINE FROMAGE DE CHEVRE JAMBON

GOAT CHEESE AND HAM TARTINE

Prep time: 5 minutes ⚜ *Cook time: 5 minutes*

UNDER 30 MINUTES

4 slices of ½-inch thick
sourdough bread

1 garlic clove, peeled

4 Rocamadour
(or 4 tiny creamy and ripened
goat cheeses)

8 thin slices of Bayonne ham
or a great prosciutto

1 teaspoon salt

1 teaspoon freshly
ground pepper

4 tablespoons green onions

MAKES 4 TARTINES · This tartine is better made with Rocamadour, a tiny, round, soft, and soooo runny goat cheese made in Périgord, the beautiful French region that also gave us foie gras, duck confit, and jambon de Bayonne, a flavorful prosciutto made in the French Basque Country. If substituting prosciutto, select what looks like the best quality product.

1. Preheat the oven on the broiler setting.

2. Rub all the slices of bread with the garlic clove. Cut the Rocamadour cheeses in half, so as to create 8 round pieces of cheese. Place the cheese rounds on the slices of bread. Shred the slices of ham into bite-size pieces and scatter over the cheese.

3. Sprinkle the salt and pepper over each tartine and place them in the oven for 2 to 5 minutes. The tartines are ready when the sides of the ham start curling up and are crispy.

4. Sprinkle the green onions on top of each tartine.

Le Petit Truc Serve with a green lettuce salad coated in Vinaigrette (page 26).

Pairing: Pair with a dry white wine.

TARTINE POIRE FOURME D'AMBERT

PEAR AND BLEU CHEESE TARTINE

Prep time: 7 minutes

Origin: Auvergne

VEGETARIAN · UNDER 30 MINUTES

½ pound Fourme d'Ambert (or a soft bleu cheese)

1 tablespoon crème fraîche or whipping cream

2 ripe pears, peeled and cut into thin slices

Juice of half a lemon

4 thick slices of sourdough bread

¼ cup walnut halves

1 tablespoon freshly ground pepper

2 tablespoons raw honey, divided

MAKES 4 TARTINES · This pear and bleu cheese tartine is great to make on the go, as it doesn't need any cooking. You can make it with any bleu cheese, but Fourme d'Ambert makes the dish even better. This cow-milk cheese is not as strong as other bleu cheeses and is a kid's favorite. Try to use fruits that are perfectly ripe and juicy.

1. In a bowl, roughly mash the cheese and the cream using a fork.

2. Place the pears on a plate and pour the lemon juice on top.

3. Spread the bleu cheese and cream mixture onto the slices of bread. Place the pear slices on top. Cover with 2 or 3 walnut halves and ground pepper, and gently drizzle about a teaspoon of honey over each tartine.

Le Petit Truc You can cover with prosciutto, coppa, or duck bacon slices. Serve with an arugula salad in Vinaigrette (page 26).

Pairing: Pair with a sweet white wine, such as chenin blanc or Sauternes.

TARTINE FOIE GRAS KAKI

PERSIMMON AND FOIE GRAS TARTINE

Prep time: 20 minutes

Origin: Southwest of France

DAIRY FREE · UNDER 30 MINUTES · CLASSIC

1 tablespoon Armagnac brandy or use your favorite local brandy

1 teaspoon cider vinegar

1 teaspoon raw honey

1 teaspoon salt

1 teaspoon freshly ground pepper

1 persimmon, ripe, peeled and diced

4 slices of sourdough bread, with walnuts, if possible

½ pound foie gras

1 teaspoon Espelette pepper

MAKES 4 TARTINES · Foie gras is such an exclusive treat it doesn't need anything to supplement it, but I must say I love this sweet and sour tartine, which uses persimmon, a fruit that is becoming more common at the farmers' markets in southwest France, where I like to spend the summers (and where foie gras is especially delicious).

1. In a bowl, mix the brandy, vinegar, honey, salt, and pepper.

2. Add the persimmon to the marinade and let it rest for 15 minutes.

3. Toast the slices of bread slightly.

4. Meanwhile, cut the foie gras into thin slices.

5. Place the foie gras on the slices of bread. Then place 1 tablespoon of the marinated persimmon on top. Season with Espelette pepper.

Le Petit Truc To cut the foie gras in even slices, let it rest at room temperature for 30 minutes before serving. When cutting, dip your knife into a bowl of boiling water after each slice. Serve with a mixed greens or arugula salad in Vinaigrette (page 26).

Pairing: Pair with a sweet white wine, such as Sauternes.

TARTINE FROMAGE BLANC RADIS

RADISH AND FRESH CHEESE TARTINE

Prep time: 7 minutes

VEGETARIAN · UNDER 30 MINUTES

4 ½-inch-thick slices of bread, preferably sourdough

¼ cup *fromage blanc* (or substitute with ⅛ cup Greek yogurt and ⅛ cup ricotta or cottage cheese)

1 tablespoon olive oil

2 tablespoons chives, finely sliced, divided

6 radishes, cut into thin slices

1 teaspoon salt

MAKES 4 TARTINES · *Fromage blanc* is a common dairy product in France that is sadly hard to find in the United States. However, I adapted the recipe for you to enjoy this simple and fresh radish tartine. Serve with a romaine lettuce salad in Vinaigrette (page 26). You can substitute with Boursin cheese, a fresh herb cheese that can sometimes be found in US supermarkets.

1. Place the slices of bread in a toaster, and brown them gently.

2. In a bowl, whisk the *fromage blanc* with the olive oil and 1 tablespoon of the chives.

3. Spread the cheese mixture onto the slices of bread. Sprinkle the radishes with salt, place on top of the cheese mixture, place the radish slices on top and sprinkle with the rest of the green onions.

Le Petit Truc Don't throw away the leaves of the radishes, as they make a great soup that's full of vitamins. Follow the Soupe à l'Oseille recipe (page 116), substituting the radish leaves for the sorrel.

CROQUE MONSIEUR BÉCHAMEL

GRILLED CHEESE AND HAM SANDWICH IN BÉCHAMEL SAUCE

Prep time: 20 minutes ✤ Cook time: 10 minutes

Origin: Paris

UNDER 30 MINUTES · CLASSIC

8 slices of sourdough bread

1 cup Sauce Béchamel (page 34)

4 slices of jambon blanc or thinly sliced cooked ham

½ cup grated cheese (Comté or Gruyère preferably, or mozzarella)

SERVES 4 · It's more than a grilled ham sandwich: Croque Monsieur is one of the top 10 things to eat while in France! This is a typical dish in any French bistro, along with its Sauce Béchamel (page 34).

1. Preheat the oven to 350°F.

2. Spread the slices of bread with Sauce Béchamel.

3. Sprinkle 2 tablespoons of grated cheese on 4 of the slices, then add a folded slice of ham, and cover with another slice of bread.

4. Cover all 4 sandwiches with Sauce Béchamel and 1 tablespoon of grated cheese.

5. Place sandwiches on a sheet pan lined with parchment paper and cook for 10 minutes.

6. Serve warm.

Le Petit Truc Serve with a simple green salad and Vinaigrette (page 26). Add a fried egg on top to make it a *croque madame!*

CROQUE MONSIEUR MAISON

BAKED GRILLED CHEESE AND HAM SANDWICH

Prep time: 5 minutes ✦ *Cook time: 10 minutes*

UNDER 30 MINUTES · CLASSIC

4 teaspoons Dijon mustard

8 slices of sourdough bread

½ cup grated cheese (preferably Gruyère or a tasty cheese like Mimolette or Comté)

4 slices of jambon blanc or thinly sliced ham

2 tablespoons butter

SERVES 4 · This *croque monsieur* recipe is not served in brasseries; it is more of a home-cooked version. It's much easier and is a little less disastrous to the calorie count.

1. Preheat the oven to 400°F.

2. Spread Dijon mustard on each slice of bread.

3. Take 4 slices, and place 2 tablespoons of grated cheese over the mustard on each slice, then add a folded slice of ham. Cover with another slice of bread, mustard side on the inside of the sandwich.

4. Spread butter on the top piece of bread. Place on a baking sheet lined with parchment paper and cook for 10 minutes.

Le Petit Truc Serve warm with a simple green lettuce salad in Vinaigrette (page 26).

PAIN PERDU

FRENCH TOAST

Prep time: 5 minutes ✦ *Cook time: 5 minutes*

VEGETARIAN · UNDER 30 MINUTES · CLASSIC

2 eggs

½ cup brown sugar,
plus ⅓ cup

1 teaspoon orange blossom
water or substitute
vanilla extract

2 cups whole milk

8 thick slices of stale
sourdough bread

1 tablespoon butter

SERVES 4 · French Toast in French is called . . . Lost Bread—Pain Perdu—because you use stale bread that would have been lost. Not really a breakfast item there, it's more a dessert or something you make for *le goûter,* the snack kids always have at 4 p.m.

1. In a bowl, break the eggs and whisk them with the brown sugar and the orange blossom water.

2. Pour the milk into another large bowl.

3. Dip each slice of bread first in the milk and then in the egg mixture. Place the soaked slices on a plate and sprinkle each one with brown sugar.

4. In a large nonstick skillet over medium heat, melt the butter. Make sure it doesn't get brown. Fry the soaked bread slices in the pan for 1 to 2 minutes on each side.

5. Serve immediately.

PAIN PERDU SALÉ

SAVORY FRENCH TOAST

Prep time: 5 minutes ✦ Cook time: 5 minutes

VEGETARIAN · UNDER 30 MINUTES · CLASSIC

2 eggs

1 tablespoon Espelette pepper
or paprika

1 cup whole milk

8 thick slices of stale bread

1 teaspoon salt

1 teaspoon freshly
ground pepper

2 tablespoons butter

½ cup grated cheese (Gruyère,
Comté, or aged Cheddar)

SERVES 4 · It's Sunday evening and you don't want to cook. My mom had a great tradition on that kind of night: Pain Perdu Salé. All you need is stale bread, eggs, milk, and cheese.

1. Break the eggs in a large bowl, add the Espelette pepper, and whisk well.

2. Pour the milk in another bowl. Dip each slice of bread first in the milk, then in the egg mixture. Place the soaked slices on a plate and sprinkle with salt and pepper.

3. In a large nonstick skillet over medium heat, melt the butter. Make sure it doesn't get brown. Fry the slices in the pan for 1 to 2 minutes on each side. The bread should never stick to the pan, so don't hesitate to add butter. Top with a tablespoon of grated cheese after flipping the bread, and let it melt.

Le Petit Truc You can substitute nutmeg for the Espelette pepper. Some also substitute tomato sauce or broth for the milk.

SIDES

CHAPTER TEN

VEGETABLES HAVE A LONG HISTORY in French cuisine. For a long time, meat was only reserved for special occasions, or special budgets—if kings and counts could feast on endless buffets of stuffed pigeons and marinated lamb, 95 percent of the population felt blessed when they could have meat once a week, on Sunday.

Recipes for sides in French cuisine all have a regional touch, using the vegetables and ingredients that are available locally: zucchini, eggplant, and tomatoes in Provence for Ratatouille (page 133), potatoes and cream for the Gratin Dauphinois (page 140), created in the harsh climate of the Alps.

Keep in mind that most of these recipes can also be served on their own, *gratins* especially. These ancestors of the casseroles consist of vegetables cooked together in the oven, in the same dish: *le plat à gratin*, usually a large rectangular ovenproof dish.

And then, there is *la pomme de terre*. Literally the apple of earth in French, the potato is one of the favorite ingredients for today's easy home-cooked meals. A gift from the Americas to Old Europe, it saved millions of people from famine, and is used in hundreds of delicious recipes, including a fried potatoes recipe that conquered the world: Frites (French fries) (page 136).

RATATOUILLE

PROVENÇAL VEGETABLE STEW

Prep time: 15 minutes ✦ Cook time: 65 minutes

Origin: Provence

DAIRY FREE · GLUTEN FREE · CLASSIC

1 tablespoon olive oil

7 ounces bacon, cut into
½-inch slices (optional)

1 onion, diced

1 bell pepper, cut into
½-inch cubes

1 large eggplant, cut into
½-inch cubes

4 zucchini, cut into
½-inch cubes

1 teaspoon salt

1 teaspoon freshly
ground pepper

1 garlic clove, peeled
and minced

1 bouquet garni (see page 13)

1 (48-ounce) can of peeled and
diced tomatoes

SERVES 4 · Don't let the Pixar movie fool you: Ratatouille is easy to make! It's all about slow cooking and herbs. I love to eat it warm, but it is also delicious served cold. If you have leftovers, Ratatouille spread on a thick slice of bread makes a great tartine.

1. In a medium French oven or cast-iron pot, heat the olive oil over medium heat. Add the bacon, cook for 1 minute, and add the onion. Cook for 5 minutes, stirring well. Add the bell pepper and cook for 5 minutes. Add the eggplant, stir well, and cook for another 5 minutes before adding the zucchini.

2. Add the salt, pepper, garlic, and bouquet garni and stir well. Then add the diced tomatoes and stir again. Turn the heat to low, cover, and cook for 45 minutes, stirring often.

Le Petit Truc Ratatouille is a perfect side dish for meat or fish or is a meal in itself when topped with a sunny-side-up egg.

Pairing: Pair with a bottle of rosé.

PETITS POIS CAROTTES

GREEN PEAS AND CARROTS

Prep time: 10 minutes ✦ *Cook time: 25 minutes*

GLUTEN FREE · CLASSIC

1 tablespoon butter

1 pound fresh peas

¼ cup lettuce, thinly chopped

4 pearl onions, peeled,
or 1 onion, minced

3 carrots, cut into
½-inch slices

1 teaspoon salt

1 teaspoon freshly
ground pepper

1½ cups chicken stock

SERVES 4 · Even better (and healthier!) than Frites (page 136), peas and carrots are a traditional side dish for red meat in France. I also found this sweet mix to be a toddler's favorite, and a great way to introduce *bébé* to the joys of vegetables.

1. In a medium saucepan, melt the butter over medium heat. Add the peas, sliced lettuce, carrots, and onions. Stir well and add the salt and pepper.

2. Pour in the chicken broth and bring to a boil over high heat. Then reduce to low heat and simmer for 25 minutes.

Le Petit Truc You can serve with poultry. For the bacon lover, cut 2 slices of bacon into ½-inch-wide strips. Brown the bacon, and then add the vegetables, cooking them in the bacon fat. This is *petits pois lardons,* another classic French dish.

PIPERADE

TOMATO AND PEPPER STEW

Prep time: 10 minutes ✦ *Cook time: 50 minutes*

Origin: Southwest of France, Basque Country

VEGETARIAN · DAIRY FREE · GLUTEN FREE · CLASSIC

½ pound sweet peppers
(preferably *piments doux*—
sweet green peppers) or
1 green bell pepper

1 tablespoon olive oil

1 bunch of green onions
or 1 onion, minced

2 garlic cloves, peeled
and minced

1 teaspoon salt

1 teaspoon freshly
ground pepper

1 teaspoon Espelette pepper

1 (48-ounce) can of diced and
peeled tomatoes

1 pound tomatoes,
peeled and diced

½ teaspoon sugar

1 egg

SERVES 4 · Everybody in southwestern France has their own family Piperade recipe. Here is how Gisele, a friend of my family, makes it at her farm. It can be served as a side dish, with fish for example, or as a dish in itself, with a thick slice of fried *jambon de Bayonne*, French prosciutto.

1. Cut the peppers into very thin slices (about ½ inch long, and ¼ inch wide).

2. Heat the olive oil in a nonstick skillet, over medium heat. Add the minced onions and the peppers. Stir well, cook for 5 minutes, then add the garlic, salt, pepper, and Espelette pepper, and cook for 5 minutes, still stirring often. Add the tomatoes and the sugar. Stir well, reduce the heat to low, and simmer for 45 minutes.

3. Right before serving, whisk the egg in a bowl, and add at the last minute into the Piperade.

Le Petit Truc Piperade is not really a Piperade without *piments doux*—sweet peppers. These small green peppers are not spicy at all and are sweeter than bell peppers. But they are hard to find outside of southwestern France. I usually use sweet peppers I find at the farmers' market or green bell pepper. You can also break 4 eggs on top of the sauce, cover the pan, and cook for 7 more minutes.

Pairing: Pair with a glass of a full-bodied red wine.

FRITES

FRENCH FRIES

Prep time: 45 minutes ✳ *Cook time: 40 minutes*

DAIRY FREE · GLUTEN FREE · UNDER 30 MINUTES · CLASSIC

2 pounds starchy potatoes
(Idaho or Russet), peeled and
cut into ⅛-inch cubes

1 cup canola oil for frying
or 1 cup beef tallow

1 tablespoon lard (optional)

SERVES 6 · How sad would life be without French fries! Frites are of course a big element of French food and have made it famous all over the world. The best you can have in France are made in northern France, where they use beef tallow for more flavor. Here is how I was taught to make them.

1. Plunge the potatoes into a large bowl of fresh water. Cover and set aside for 30 minutes. Drain in a colander and pat dry thoroughly with a cotton cloth. Divide the potatoes into 3 batches of equal size.

2. Fill a large saucepan with oil (or the beef tallow and lard combination if possible), and bring it to 300°F. Put ⅓ of the potatoes in a frying basket and plunge them into the saucepan for 7 minutes. Then take them out, put them back in the dried colander, and do the same for the 2 other batches. Let them cool down for about 15 minutes.

3. Prepare 2 large bowls with a paper towel covering the bottom. Bring the oil or the fat to 350°F. Plunge the first batch of potatoes in for around 3 minutes (they must be perfectly golden) then put the fries in a bowl. Then put them in the second bowl and change the paper towel in the first bowl before frying the second batch of the potatoes. Do the same for the rest of the fries.

Le Petit Truc Serve immediately with salt on the table for guests to add to their liking.

PURÉE DE POMMES DE TERRE

FRENCH MASHED POTATOES

Prep time: 10 minutes ✛ *Cook time: 30 minutes*

VEGETARIAN · GLUTEN FREE · CLASSIC

**2 pounds potatoes
(Russet or Yukon Gold),
peeled and chopped into
large chunks**

**1 tablespoon salt,
plus 1 teaspoon, divided**

1 cup whole milk

2 tablespoons butter, diced

1 teaspoon ground nutmeg

**1 teaspoon freshly
ground pepper**

SERVES 6 · Mashed potatoes *à la française* are often served with roasted chicken or a nice red meat. At home when I was a child, it was always on the menu on Wednesdays, when French kids didn't go to school.

1. Fill a large saucepan with water, add 1 tablespoon of salt and the potatoes, and bring to a boil over high heat. Boil for 25 minutes. A knife blade should be able to sink into the potatoes easily. Drain the potatoes in a colander, and mash them with a vegetable mill.

2. In a medium saucepan, warm the milk over medium heat. Stop before the boiling point, then pour slowly over the potatoes, stirring constantly with a wooden spoon. Add the butter, nutmeg, remaining teaspoon of salt, and pepper, stirring until smooth.

3. Serve immediately.

Le Petit Truc Never use a blender to mash the potatoes. The traditional French way calls for using a food mill. The Moulinex food mills are passed down from one generation to the other!

TOMATES À LA PROVENÇALE

PROVENÇAL TOMATOES

Prep time: 5 minutes ✦ *Cook time: 20 minutes*

Origin: Provence

VEGAN · VEGETARIAN · DAIRY FREE · UNDER 30 MINUTES

8 medium round
tomatoes, sliced in half

1 teaspoon salt

1 teaspoon freshly
ground pepper

4 garlic cloves, peeled
and minced

4 tablespoons bread crumbs

4 tablespoons finely chopped
fresh parsley

2 tablespoons thyme

1 tablespoon olive oil

SERVES 4 · The perfect side dish for a barbecue, these roasted tomatoes from Provence call for a glass of chilled rosé and some delicious grilled meat or fish. They also use herbs that are classic in southern France, and often called *herbes de Provence* in France.

1. Add the salt, and the pepper to the tomatoes. Place them on a large plate with the seasoned-side down so the water soaks out. Set aside for 15 minutes.

2. In a small bowl, combine the garlic with the bread crumbs, parsley, and thyme.

3. Preheat the oven to 400°F.

4. Place a sheet of parchment paper over a baking sheet. Then place the halved tomatoes on the parchment paper. Using a tablespoon, place the herb and garlic mixture over each tomato. Sprinkle bread crumbs on top.

5. Pour 1 tablespoon of olive oil over the tomatoes and put in the oven for 20 minutes.

Le Petit Truc This recipe can also be made in a nonstick skillet. Heat 1 tablespoon of olive oil over moderate heat, then place the halved tomatoes inside facing the bottom for 2 minutes. Flip them back, add the parsley and garlic, and simmer for 10 minutes.

Pairing: Pair with a glass of chilled rosé.

GRATIN DAUPHINOIS

POTATO GRATIN

Prep time: 15 minutes ✦ Cook time: 35 minutes

Origin: Alps

VEGETARIAN · GLUTEN FREE · CLASSIC

1 garlic clove, peeled

1 teaspoon butter, plus
3 tablespoons, diced

1 cup milk

3 cups whipping cream

1 teaspoon ground nutmeg

3 pounds potatoes, peeled and
cut into thin slices

1 teaspoon salt

1 teaspoon freshly
ground pepper

SERVES 4 · Potatoes *au gratin* are a typical family dish, especially during the winter. The classical recipe calls for only milk and cream, but lots of French people also love to add cheese in it, in which case it is called a *gratin savoyard*. They are great with roast beef, a roasted chicken, or on their own with a green salad in Vinaigrette (page 26).

1. Rub the garlic clove inside a large baking dish. Butter the dish with 1 teaspoon of butter. Reserve.

2. Pour the milk and cream into a medium saucepan, and add the nutmeg. Bring to a boil over high heat, stir well, then add the potato slices. Reduce the heat to low, and simmer for 10 minutes.

3. Preheat the oven to 350°F. Using a slotted spoon, take the potato slices out of the saucepan and place them in the baking dish. Season with salt and pepper.

4. Turn the heat under the saucepan to high and reduce the milk and cream combination by half. Pour over the potatoes, and place 3 tablespoons of diced butter on top. Put in the oven and cook for 20 minutes.

5. Serve lukewarm.

Le Petit Truc To reheat the gratin, add some cream and milk to retain the moisture.

GRATIN DE COURGETTES

ZUCCHINI GRATIN

Prep time: 7 minutes ✦ *Cook time: 45 minutes*

VEGETARIAN · GLUTEN FREE

3 eggs

3 tablespoons crème fraîche or whipping cream

1 teaspoon salt

1 teaspoon freshly ground pepper

5 zucchini, peeled and sliced thinly

3 tablespoons mint, minced

½ cup fresh goat cheese

SERVES 4 AS A WHOLE DISH, 6 AS A SIDE DISH · This mint, goat cheese, and zucchini casserole has the flavors of Corsica, the French island in the Mediterranean where mint is often used in savory dishes. This gratin is delicious with a roasted chicken, grilled meat, or fish, but it can also be a vegetarian main course.

1. Preheat your oven to 350°F.

2. In a large bowl, whisk the eggs. Add the cream, salt, and pepper.

3. Place the zucchini and mint in a large ovenproof dish. Crumble the goat cheese evenly on top.

4. Pour the egg mixture on top. Bake for 45 minutes.

Le Petit Truc You can substitute the mint with thyme, rosemary, or fresh oregano. Feta can also be a nice topping.

Pairing: Pair with rosé or a dry white wine.

GRATIN DE PÂTES

FRENCH MAC AND CHEESE

Prep time: 10 minutes ✦ Cook time: 35 minutes

CLASSIC

½ pound uncooked
pasta or 1 pound cooked
pasta (macaroni is better,
of course!)

1 teaspoon salt

½ pound button mushrooms,
thinly sliced

1 tablespoon finely chopped
fresh parsley

2 slices of ham, cut into
½-inch squares (optional)

10 cherry tomatoes, halved

2 tablespoons butter, divided

1 cup Sauce Béchamel
(page 34)

½ cup grated cheese (Gruyère,
Comté, or Cheddar)

SERVES 4 · I was amazed to discover that mac and cheese was such a big thing in the United States. It reminded me of the dish my grandmother and my mother used to make from scratch when they had leftover pasta. You will see that the French macaroni and cheese is rich, but far less so than the American version. Also, it includes vegetables (a great way to have kids eat their veggies). You can serve with roasted chicken or on its own.

1. For uncooked pasta, cook ½ pound of macaroni in salted boiling water. Drain. If using leftover pasta, proceed to the next step.

2. Preheat the oven to 400°F.

3. In a small saucepan, melt 1 tablespoon of butter over medium heat, add the mushrooms and the parsley, and cook for 5 minutes, stirring well.

4. Use the remaining tablespoon of butter to grease a large casserole dish. Pour the pasta in it, and mix with the mushrooms, the ham, and the halved tomatoes. Combine so that every ingredient is spread evenly. Pour the Sauce Béchamel on the pasta. Sprinkle the grated cheese on top. Put the dish in the oven and cook uncovered for 25 minutes.

Le Petit Truc In the winter, I also like to use the same technique with blanched cauliflower (see page 19) instead of tomatoes and mushrooms. Serve warm with a romaine lettuce salad in Vinaigrette (page 26).

TIAN PROVENÇAL

PROVENÇAL VEGETABLE CASSEROLE

Prep time: 15 minutes ✛ Cook time: 100 minutes

Origin: Provence

VEGAN · VEGETARIAN · DAIRY FREE · GLUTEN FREE · CLASSIC

2 medium onions,
thinly sliced

2 tablespoons olive oil,
divided

4 tomatoes

3 zucchini

1 eggplant

2 tablespoons thyme

1 tablespoon rosemary

1 teaspoon salt

1 teaspoon freshly
ground pepper

5 garlic cloves, unpeeled

SERVES 4 · Straight from the South of France and a specialty of Provence, this is the ultimate summer side dish. You're supposed to make it with all the vegetables you can find at the farmers' market during the summer. This casserole is great on its own or with grilled meat or fish.

1. Preheat the oven to 350°F.

2. Put the onions in a large baking dish. Add a tablespoon of olive oil, stir the onion slices, and spread them all over the bottom of the dish, so that they cover it completely. Put in the oven for 10 minutes.

3. Cut the tomatoes, zucchini, and eggplant into thin slices. All slices should be about the same size, so if the eggplant is too wide, cut it accordingly.

4. Take the dish out of the oven. Let it cool a little, then start layering the slices of vegetables on the onions: one slice tomato, one slice zucchini, one slice eggplant, then another slice of tomato, etc.

5. Sprinkle thyme and rosemary, salt and pepper, and add the garlic cloves in different places throughout the dish. Pour the remaining tablespoon of olive oil over the vegetables and put in the oven for 90 minutes.

Le Petit Truc For even more flavor, use finely sliced green onions and all the fresh herbs you can find (oregano, mint, parsley, cilantro, etc.).

EAU NON POTABLE

FISH & SEAFOOD

CHAPTER ELEVEN

IT ONLY TAKES A FEW SECONDS of looking at a map of France to understand why fish is so important in French cuisine: there is water everywhere! The country is surrounded by sea: La mer du Nord in the North, the Atlantic Ocean on the West, and the Mediterranean in the south. Plus all the beautiful rivers, home to fish (and frogs) often used in traditional French cooking. In a Catholic country like France, fish was also traditionally on the menu on Fridays, when Catholics were not supposed to eat meat. And don't forget, when eating at a super fancy restaurant, there should be special knives for fish, too!

The following recipes try to encapsulate the many ways the French like to eat fish and other seafood. It can be the Moules Marinières (page 152) you have while vacationing at the seaside, or the aïoli you share with family in Provence. Now a much more coveted meal because of its scarcity and price, fish used to be a common meal—ask any French person about eating at the school cafeteria, and he or she will probably remember fondly how they were always serving Brandade de Morue (page 157) on Fridays.

SOLE MEUNIÈRE

LEMON AND BUTTER SOLE

Prep time: 5 minutes ✷ Cook time: 5 minutes

Origin: Paris

UNDER 30 MINUTES · CLASSIC

½ cup flour

4 sole fillets, ½ pound each

1 teaspoon freshly
ground pepper

1 teaspoon salt

3 tablespoons butter, divided

Juice of 2 lemons

1 lemon, cut into thin slices

1 tablespoon minced
fresh parsley

SERVES 4 · A must for every Parisian bistro menu, the Sole Meunière is a sole cooked like a miller would cook it: with flour! Add lemon and butter to the mix, and you have fish fillets so tender and sweet that kids love to eat them. And it's so fast!

1. Pour the flour into a large dish.

2. Season the sole fillets with salt and pepper, and place them in the flour. Flip so that every side is coated with flour.

3. In a large nonstick skillet, melt 1 tablespoon of butter over medium heat, let it slightly brown: it must get the "noisette" color, like a hazelnut.

4. Place the sole fillets in the skillet, cook for 1 minute on one side, then flip on the other side to cook for another minute. Using a wooden spatula, take the sole fillets out of the skillet, and place them on 4 plates. Add the remaining 2 tablespoons of butter to the skillet, let it turn slightly brown (noisette) then add the juices of the lemons. Stir well, and pour on the soles.

5. Serve warm, topped with lemon slices and parsley.

Le Petit Truc You can use the *meunière* system to cook other white fish. Serve with a bowl of white rice or tiny boiled potatoes.

Pairing: Pair with white wine, like sauvignon blanc or Pessac Leognan, for instance.

SAUMON À L'OSEILLE

SALMON IN SORREL SAUCE

Prep time: 5 minutes ✦ *Cook time: 5 minutes*

GLUTEN FREE · UNDER 30 MINUTES · CLASSIC

FOR THE SORREL SAUCE

1 cup white wine

1 bay leaf

3 peppercorns

3 small shallots, minced

2 cups crème fraîche
or Mexican crema

1 pound fresh sorrel, minced

FOR THE SALMON

4 salmon fillets, about
1 inch thick

1 teaspoon salt

1 teaspoon freshly
ground pepper

SERVES 4 · This salmon in sorrel sauce is now a classic of French cuisine. The history of its introduction to French cooking is famous: In the 1960s, when the Troisgros brothers, two legendary Michelin-starred chefs, put it on their menu, it was so different and delicious that it is said to have launched a movement called *nouvelle cuisine* that revolutionized French food for a generation of French chefs.

TO MAKE THE SORREL SAUCE

1. Pour the white wine into a medium saucepan, and add the bay leaf, peppercorns, and shallots. Bring to a boil over high heat, until the liquid reduces by more than half.

2. Add the cream, stir well, and bring to a boil, cook for 2 minutes, then throw the sorrel in, stir immediately with a wooden spoon, and remove from the heat.

TO MAKE THE SALMON

1. Sprinkle the salmon fillets with salt and pepper.

2. Heat a large nonstick skillet on high, place the salmon fillets in the pan, and cook them 15 seconds on each side. That's it! The edges will be cooked, and the center kind of raw, but that's what you want!

3. Pour the sorrel sauce in dinner plates, quickly top with the salmon, and serve immediately.

Le Petit Truc To eat the real authentic recipe, you can still go to the 3-Michelin-starred Troisgros restaurant in Roanne, where the son of one of the brothers still makes one of the best cuisines in the world. He deliberately took the salmon off the menu but still makes it on demand. Just ask!

Pairing: Pair with a dry young white wine, Chablis, Cour-Cheverny, or chardonnay.

AÏOLI DE POISSONS

FISH AND AÏOLI

Prep time: 20 minutes ✤ *Cook time: 20 minutes*

Origin: Provence, South of France

DAIRY FREE · GLUTEN FREE · CLASSIC

FOR THE FISH AND VEGETABLES

6 salted cod fillets

8 medium potatoes, unpeeled

1 pound carrots, peeled

1 small cauliflower

1 pound organic zucchini, unpeeled, cut into 1-inch slices

2 medium leeks, green part discarded

1 pound French beans, trimmed at the ends

4 eggs

FOR THE AÏOLI

6 garlic cloves, peeled

1 teaspoon salt

2 egg yolks

1 teaspoon freshly ground pepper

⅓ cup olive oil

SERVES 6 · Aïoli is more than a sauce. It's a whole dish, and a symbol of Provençal cuisine and its generosity. Prepare the aïoli for a big table of guests, friends, and/or family, who gather for the simple and gourmet pleasure of steamed fish, vegetables, and an amazing garlicky sauce.

TO MAKE THE FISH AND VEGETABLES

1. A day before, put the salted cod fillets in a large bowl of fresh water.

2. The next day, fill a large saucepan with water, put the potatoes in, bring to a boil, and cook for 20 minutes. Boil the carrots, cauliflower, zucchini, leeks, and French beans for 15 minutes in a separate saucepan.

3. Boil the eggs for 10 minutes. Peel and halve them.

4. Fill a large saucepan with water, bring to a boil, and add the salted cod fillets. Reduce the heat to low and cook for 10 minutes. Using a slotted spoon, take the fish out. Place on a serving plate, cover it and reserve.

5. Place the vegetables and the eggs in a serving dish, and the fish in another one.

TO MAKE THE AÏOLI

Use a garlic clove to rub on the surface of a medium bowl. Put the other cloves in a mortar with a teaspoon of salt. Crush and pour them in the bowl. Add the egg yolks and the pepper, and whisk steadily. Pour the olive oil little by little, whisking without stopping until the sauce is thick.

Le Petit Truc Put the aïoli on the table. Guests should help themselves and add as much aïoli as they want to their plate.

Pairing: Pair with rosé or a dry white wine.

MOULES MARINIÈRES

MUSSELS IN WHITE WINE

Prep time: 10 minutes + Cook time: 15 minutes

Origin: West of France

GLUTEN FREE · UNDER 30 MINUTES · CLASSIC

2 tablespoons butter

4 medium shallots, minced

2 garlic cloves

1 bouquet garni (see page 13)

1 teaspoon salt

1 teaspoon freshly
ground pepper

2 cups white wine
(sauvignon blanc)

3 pounds mussels, scrubbed,
beards removed

3 tablespoons roughly
chopped fresh parsley

SERVES 4 · You're sitting on a sunny terrace overlooking a French harbor. Boats are coming in and out, to fish or have fun. There's a nice bottle of chilled white wine on the table, and of course, you're having the perfect dish to eat on such a great moment: Moules Marinières! Good news: even if you're stuck at home and far from the sea, you can still make this delicious and super easy dish! Just don't forget the main element that makes this dish even better: the Frites (page 136) that accompany it!

1. Melt the butter over medium heat, in a very large pot. Add the minced shallots, stir well, and cook for 2 minutes.

2. Peel the garlic and crush it with the side of a knife. Add to the pot, stir well, and cook for 5 minutes, then add the bouquet garni, salt, and pepper.

3. Pour the white wine into the pot, and add the mussels. Cook over high heat, until the mussels are all opened. Stir well, remove from the heat.

4. Add the fresh parsley leaves at the last minute and serve immediately.

Le Petit Truc When you buy the mussels, make sure that they are shiny, and tightly closed. Then clean them in fresh water thoroughly to make sure all little stones (or sometimes miniature crabs!) are gone.

Pairing: Pair with a nice blond beer or a dry young white wine (one that hasn't aged too much), like a Muscadet.

BOUILLABAISSE DE MARSEILLE

FISH STEW

Prep time: 15 minutes ✦ *Cook time: 30 minutes*

Origin: Provence, South of France

DAIRY FREE · CLASSIC

2 tablespoons olive oil,
plus 1 cup, divided

1 onion, minced

1 small (14-ounce) can
diced tomatoes

7 garlic cloves, divided

1 fennel, cut into ½-inch cubes

1 bouquet garni (page 13)

½ teaspoon saffron threads

1 teaspoon salt

1 teaspoon freshly
ground pepper

8 cups of white fish stock,
plus ⅓ cup, divided

1 pound mussels, scrubbed,
beards removed

4 pounds of white fish
fillets (seabass, monkfish,
red snapper, or turbot)

1 slice of stale bread

1 egg yolk

SERVES 4 · Bouillabaisse is a legendary fish stew, and something like a national specialty in Marseille, the second-biggest city in France. It's traditionally made with local Mediterranean fish (what the fishermen brought back that morning).

1. In a large pot, heat 2 tablespoons of olive oil over high heat. Add the minced onions, stir well for 2 minutes, then add the diced tomatoes, and 4 cloves of minced garlic. Reduce the heat to medium and cook for 5 minutes, stirring occasionally. Add the fennel, bouquet garni, saffron, salt, and pepper.

2. Pour in 8 cups of white fish stock, bring to a boil over high heat, then reduce the heat to low, cover, and simmer for 5 minutes.

3. Add the mussels, cover and cook for 5 minutes, then add the fish fillets, cover again and cook for 15 minutes.

4. Meanwhile prepare the *rouille* sauce: Using a ladle, pour ⅓ cup of white fish stock in a soup plate, and soak the bread in it. Put in a blender with 3 peeled garlic cloves. Pour the mixture into a medium bowl, add an egg yolk, whisk, and slowly add the olive oil, until you get a thick sauce.

5. Serve the mussels and fish in a large bowl. Pour the broth into a soup bowl, and bring the *rouille* to the table. Guests should help themselves to fish, broth, and *rouille* all together.

Pairing: Pair with rosé or a dry white wine.

BAR EN CROÛTE DE SEL

SEABASS IN SALT CRUST

Prep time: 5 minutes ✦ *Cook time: 45 minutes*

DAIRY FREE · GLUTEN FREE

1 (3-pound) sea bass, cleaned with head and tail intact

1 tablespoon rosemary

1 tablespoon thyme

1 fennel stalk

3 pounds coarse salt

3 egg whites

SERVES 4 · Bringing to the table a whole fish covered with a huge coat of salt is always very dramatic, but what your guests will not know is how easy it is to do! One of the best ways to slow cook a fish.

1. Preheat the oven to 400°F.

2. Clean the fish, pat it dry, and stuff the rosemary, thyme, and fennel into the cavity.

3. In a large bowl, combine the salt and egg whites. Whisk well, then pour ⅓ of the salt mixture in a large baking dish. Place the fish on the salt bed.

4. Pour the rest of the salt over the fish. The salt layer should be about ½ inch thick. Put in the oven and cook for 45 minutes. Bring the fish to the table, and break the crust with a knife.

Le Petit Truc Serve with boiled potatoes or a Tian Provençal (page 143).

Pairing: Pair with dry white wine.

CUISSES DE GRENOUILLES

FROG LEGS

Prep time: 5 minutes ✦ *Cook time: 20 minutes*

Origin: Burgundy

UNDER 30 MINUTES · CLASSIC

30 frog legs

1 teaspoon salt

2 teaspoons freshly
ground pepper

1 cup flour

⅔ cup butter, cut into
½-inch cubes

3 garlic cloves, peeled
and minced

4 tablespoons finely chopped
fresh parsley

SERVES 4 · Fried frog legs is a delicacy that is becoming hard to find in France because frogs are getting scarce in Les Dombes, where they used to be found. Now the French have to import frogs from the state of Florida! Discover this crunchy delight that has given us the nickname of "Froggies" from our British neighbors. This is the traditional frog legs recipe using *persillade*, a parsley butter.

1. Clean the frog legs under fresh water, pat them dry, and season them with salt and pepper.

2. Pour the flour into a large dish, coat the frog legs thoroughly with it, and set aside.

3. Working in batches, melt the butter in a large nonstick skillet over medium heat. Add the frog legs. When the butter turns light brown, flip the legs onto the other side.

4. Add the garlic and parsley, stir, and cover the skillet. Cook for 5 minutes on low heat.

5. Serve immediately.

Le Petit Truc Serve with plenty of napkins, as you can only eat frog legs with your hands!

Pairing: Pair with a white Burgundy wine.

BRANDADE DE MORUE

SALT COD BRANDADE

Prep time: 15 minutes (prepare overnight) ✷ *Cook time: 45 minutes*

GLUTEN FREE · CLASSIC

2 pounds salt cod, unsalted

2 pounds potatoes, peeled

2 tablespoons olive oil

2 medium onions, chopped

2 garlic cloves, peeled and minced

½ cup whole milk

1 teaspoon freshly ground pepper

SERVES 4 · Salt cod is a common fish in French cuisine. Storing it in salt allowed for better preservation in the days before refrigeration. Brandade is a sort of fish casserole—a shepherd's pie with salt cod in it.

1. In a large bowl of fresh water, soak the salt cod for at least 24 hours.

2. Preheat the oven to 350°F.

3. Fill a large saucepan with water and add the cod and the potatoes. Bring to a boil and cook for 20 minutes. Remove the potatoes and fish with a slotted spoon and shred the fish into bite-size pieces. Remove all of the bones from the fish. Mash the potatoes with a fork and set aside.

4. In a nonstick skillet, heat the olive oil over medium heat. Add the onions and cook for 3 minutes. Add the garlic and the shredded cod. Stir for 3 minutes over low heat.

5. Add the potatoes to the skillet. Stir well, slowly pour in the milk, and stir again.

6. Pour everything into a casserole dish and flatten it with a wooden spatula. Sprinkle pepper all over the top. Put the dish in the oven and cook for 15 minutes.

7. Serve on a plate immediately.

Le Petit Truc You can also make this recipe with fresh salmon or haddock. Serve with a green lettuce salad in Vinaigrette (page 26).

POULTRY

CHAPTER TWELVE

LA VOLAILLE—POULTRY—is essential in a French diet. Think about a typical French farm, and you see chickens running in the background—at least that's how it was at my grandparents! Easier to breed and cheaper to buy, chicken was a staple even for the poor. A French king, Henri IV, is even famous for setting a culinary goal for his reign: that every French family could have chicken on the table every Sunday.

French chefs have all found their own way of cooking it, from Paul Bocuse's *Poularde truffée en vessie* (a fat hen stuffed with black truffles and cooked in a pouch) to Georges Blanc's *Poulet de Bresse à la crème* (with crème fraîche and morels).

Every region in France has its recipe: with crème fraîche in Normandy (Poulet à la Normande, page 166), and tomatoes and pepper in the Basque Country (Poulet Basquaise page, 168). My grandmother's favorite was Coq au Vin (page 164), a hen or rooster in red wine sauce.

But poultry includes more than chicken, and the French eat it all! Duck is also a favorite, from Canard à l'Orange (page 167) to *Magret de Canard,* and capons and turkeys are almost always on the menu for Christmas.

POULET RÔTI

ROASTED CHICKEN

*Prep time: 5 minutes * Cook time: 1 hour*

DAIRY FREE · GLUTEN FREE · CLASSIC

1 (3-pound) whole chicken

1 teaspoon freshly
ground pepper

2 tablespoons salt, divided

½ onion

1 lemon

1 tablespoon fresh sage

1 tablespoon thyme

6 carrots

4 garlic cloves

SERVES 6 · It's the simplest and maybe the best dinner for family or friends. Poulet Rôti always makes everybody happy (at least if they eat meat!) and is so easy to make. Here is the recipe to get that special caramelized skin and perfect perfume you can smell at any French farmers' market, where there always is a rotisserie—a roasted chicken stand. My favorite part of the recipe: the confit garlic!

1. Take your chicken out of the fridge at least an hour before cooking, so that the meat will be at room temperature.

2. Preheat the oven to 450°F.

3. Season the inside of the chicken with the pepper and 1 tablespoon of salt. Place the onion, lemon, sage, and thyme in the chicken cavity.

4. Place the carrots in a large baking pan. Place the chicken on top, and season generously with salt. Hide the garlic cloves among the carrots. Cook for 1 hour.

5. Serve the chicken with the carrots and the confit garlic.

Le Petit Truc Serve with Purée de Pommes de Terre (page 137) or a green lettuce salad in Vinaigrette (page 26). You can use the carcass to make Bouillon de Volaille (page 33).

Pairing: Pair with an acidic white wine from the Loire Valley or a riesling.

POULE AU POT

CHICKEN STEW

Prep time: 15 minutes ✦ Cook time: 4 hours

CLASSIC

FOR THE CHICKEN AND VEGETABLES

1 (6-pound) hen or fat chicken

1 onion

4 cloves

6 carrots, halved

4 turnips, halved

3 leeks, green part discarded, cut into 2 chunks

1 teaspoon salt

1 teaspoon peppercorns

1 bouquet garni (see page 13)

FOR THE SAUCE

2 tablespoons butter

2 tablespoons flour

1 cup broth, from the chicken and vegetables

SERVES 6 · This could be France's answer to chicken soup. Traditionally made with an old hen, it is equally good with a large, fat, young chicken.

TO MAKE THE CHICKEN AND VEGETABLES

1. Fill a large stove pot with cold water and place the hen or chicken into it. Stick the cloves into the onion and add to the pot. Heat slowly and simmer for 1 hour. Skim off the fat.

2. Add the carrots, turnips, leeks, salt, peppercorns, and bouquet garni to the pot. Simmer over low heat for 3 hours and skim off the fat again.

3. Fifteen minutes before serving, make the white sauce (see below).

4. Remove the hen from the pot and place on a serving dish (the meat should come apart naturally). Place the vegetables around the hen and pour the sauce over it.

TO MAKE THE SAUCE

Melt the butter in a small saucepan over medium heat. Add the flour and stir until combined into a paste. With a ladle, remove 1 cup of broth from the pot. Pour the broth slowly over the butter and flour. Whisk well over medium heat for 10 minutes or until it thickens.

Le Petit Truc Serve with white rice. Reserve the leftover broth to cook with.

Pairing: Pair with a young red wine, such as Beaujolais or pinot noir.

POULET MARENGO

CHICKEN WITH TOMATO AND MUSHROOMS

Prep time: 15 minutes ✣ Cook time: 60 minutes

DAIRY FREE · GLUTEN FREE · CLASSIC

2 tablespoons olive oil

1 onion, minced

4 chicken legs, halved

½ pound carrots, cut into 1-inch chunks

½ pound button mushrooms, minced

1 garlic clove, peeled and diced

1 bottle white wine

1 (28-ounce) can diced tomatoes

1 bay leaf

1 bouquet garni (see page 13)

2 cloves

Peel of 1 orange

1 teaspoon salt

1 teaspoon freshly ground pepper

SERVES 4 · Legend has it that this recipe was invented by Napoleon's chef at the Battle of Marengo in 1800. The troops were extremely hungry, and the cook decided to feed them with whatever he could find around him: chicken, tomatoes, mushrooms, and white wine. So if they could cook it on the battlefield, making this delicious chicken at home should be easy!

1. Heat the olive oil in a large French oven or cast-iron pot over medium heat. Add the onion, cook for 2 minutes, then add the chicken legs. Brown them on all sides. Lower the heat and cook for 5 minutes. Add the carrots and cook for 2 minutes. Add the mushrooms and garlic, and cook for another 5 minutes.

2. Pour in the white wine and bring to a boil. Add the diced tomatoes and their juice. Add the bay leaf, bouquet garni, cloves, orange peel, salt, and pepper. Reduce the heat to low and simmer for an hour. Use a slotted spoon to remove the peel, cloves, and bouquet garni out before serving.

Le Petit Truc You can use the same technique to make *Veau Marengo*: substitute chicken with 1 pound of stew veal cut into 1-inch cubes (or osso bucco), and simmer for 2 hours.

Pairing: Pair with a white wine, Bourgogne for instance.

COQ AU VIN

ROOSTER IN RED WINE

Prep time: 15 minutes ✦ Cook time: 2 hours and 30 minutes

Origin: Loire Valley

GLUTEN FREE · CLASSIC

1 tablespoon butter

4 ounces bacon, cut into
½-inch-wide strips

2 onions, minced

1 (6-pound) rooster or hen,
cut into chunks

3 carrots, peeled and cut
into ½-inch chunks

1 bottle strong red wine (like
sauvignon or malbec)

2 garlic cloves, peeled
and minced

1 bouquet garni (see page 13)

1 teaspoon salt

1 teaspoon freshly
ground pepper

4 cloves

1 pound button
mushrooms, sliced

SERVES 6 · You don't need a rooster to make this delicious dish, but red wine is essential. Though originally created to cook poultry with dense meat like rooster, this recipe can be made with a large, fat chicken. Slow cooking and perfumed red wine make all the difference.

1. In a large French oven or cast-iron pot, melt the butter over medium heat. Add the bacon and cook for 2 minutes. Add the minced onion and stir well until the onions become translucent.

2. Add the chicken or rooster pieces and brown them on each side for 5 minutes. Add the carrots, and slowly pour in the red wine. Add the garlic, bouquet garni, salt, and pepper.

3. Stick the cloves into an onion and add it to the pot.

4. Bring to a boil, cover, and simmer for at least 2 hours.

5. Thirty minutes before serving, add the mushrooms and continue simmering.

Le Petit Truc Some people like to add ¼ cup of cognac and flambé it. Serve warm with small boiled potatoes or fresh pasta.

Pairing: Pair with a red Bourgogne.

POULET À LA NORMANDE

CHICKEN IN APPLE, CIDER, AND CREAM

Prep time: 15 minutes ✦ *Cook time: 1 hour*

Origin: Normandy

GLUTEN FREE

1 tablespoon butter

4 ounces bacon, cut into ½-inch slices

4 chicken thighs

4 chicken drumsticks

2 apples, peeled, halved, cored, and quartered

½ pound button mushrooms, diced

10 tiny spring onions or 1 onion, minced

1 bottle cider

1 teaspoon salt

1 teaspoon freshly ground pepper

¾ cup crème fraîche or whipping cream

SERVES 4 · Apple trees and beautiful cows are everywhere in the green hills of Normandy. The butter, crème fraîche, apples, and cider in this simple yet delicious chicken recipe come from this beautiful region. This sweet dish is particularly loved by children.

1. In a medium French oven or cast-iron pot, melt the butter over medium heat. Add the bacon and cook for 2 minutes. Add the chicken thighs and drumsticks, and brown them on each side. Lower the heat and cook for 5 minutes, stirring well.

2. Add the apples and brown them on each side. Add the mushrooms, onions, cider, salt, and pepper and stir well.

3. Bring to a boil over high heat. Reduce heat and simmer for 45 minutes.

4. Fifteen minutes before serving, add the cream, stir well, and cover again. Serve immediately.

Le Petit Truc Try using a French cider such as *cidre brut,* which is less sweet and tastier than other ciders.

Pairing: Pair with a hard cider.

CANARD À L'ORANGE

ORANGE DUCK

Prep time: 15 minutes ✦ Cook time: 2 hours

GLUTEN FREE · CLASSIC

Peel of 2 oranges

½ cup Grand Marnier
(or triple sec)

1 tablespoon butter

1 (4-pound) duck, cut into
chunks, or 4 duck legs

⅛ cup cider or white wine
vinegar

¼ cup sugar

4 cups orange juice

1 cup white wine

4 cups water

1 bouquet garni (see page 13)

1 teaspoon salt

1 teaspoon freshly
ground pepper

SERVES 4 · *Un grand classique*, orange duck is a typical dish of the *cuisine bourgeoise*, the fine-cooking dining dishes that were served in good restaurants or good families. Serve with white rice or sautéed potatoes.

1. In a small saucepan filled with boiling water, blanch the orange peels for 2 minutes (see page 19, for more on blanching). Remove the peels from the water. Fill a medium bowl with Grand Marnier. Add the peels and marinate while you prepare the duck.

2. In a French oven or cast-iron pot, melt the butter over medium heat. Add the duck and brown on all sides.

3. In a medium saucepan over medium heat, mix the vinegar and sugar. Let the mixture caramelize without stirring. Add the orange juice and simmer for 10 minutes.

4. Pour the orange sauce onto the duck and add the white wine and 4 cups of water. Add the bouquet garni, salt, and pepper. Cover and simmer for 1½ hours.

5. Thirty minutes before serving, add the Grand Marnier and the orange peels, cover, and continue simmering.

Le Petit Truc The best restaurant to have Canard à l'Orange is Lasserre in Paris, close to the Champs-Elysees. The restaurant's founder, chef René Lasserre, is said to have revolutionized the recipe.

Pairing: Pair with a sweet white wine, such as Monbazillac or Jurançon.

POULET BASQUAISE

TOMATO AND PEPPER CHICKEN

Prep time: 10 minutes ✦ Cook time: 1 hour and 30 minutes

Origin: Southwest of France, French Basque Country

DAIRY FREE · GLUTEN FREE · CLASSIC

1 tablespoon olive oil

1 onion, minced

4 chicken legs

1 tablespoon Espelette pepper

1 red bell pepper, seeded and cut into ½-inch slices

1 garlic clove, peeled and minced

1 (28-ounce) can diced tomatoes

1 teaspoon salt

1 teaspoon freshly ground pepper

1 bottle white wine

SERVES 4 · A classic recipe from the Basque Country, in southwestern France, this chicken and tomato stew typically uses a local spice called Espelette pepper. If you can't find it, you can substitute with paprika and a hint of cayenne pepper. This dish is all about tomato and a hint of spice.

1. In a medium French oven or cast-iron pot, heat the oil over medium heat. Add the onion and cook for 3 minutes or until translucent. Add the chicken legs, browning them for 5 minutes on each side. Add the Espelette pepper.

2. Add the bell pepper and cook for 3 minutes. Add the garlic clove, and pour in the diced tomatoes and their juice. Add the salt and pepper, and stir well.

3. Pour in the white wine and bring to a boil over high heat. Cover and reduce the heat to low. Simmer for 1 hour.

Le Petit Truc Serve with a bowl of white rice or small boiled potatoes.

Pairing: Pair with a full-bodied red wine, such as cabernet sauvignon.

MAGRETS DE CANARD AUX POMMES SARLARDAISES

DUCK BREAST AND SAUTÉED POTATOES

Prep time: 15 minutes ✦ *Cook time: 25 minutes*

Origin: Southwest of France

DAIRY FREE · GLUTEN FREE

1 pound potatoes,
(preferably Yukon gold),
peeled and cut into thin slices

4 duck breasts

2 teaspoons salt, divided

2 teaspoons freshly ground
pepper, divided

1 teaspoon Espelette pepper
or paprika

6 garlic cloves, peeled
and minced

2 tablespoons minced
fresh parsley

SERVES 4 · This one-pot recipe marries two amazing ingredients: duck breast and potatoes. It's a simple and very *gourmand* way to enjoy duck, and to discover the best sautéed potatoes in my opinion: those fried in duck fat.

1. Place the potato slices in a large bowl filled with cold water.

2. Place the duck breasts on a cutting board, fat facing up. With a cutting knife, cut slits in the fat in a diamond pattern. Make sure not to cut into the meat. Flip the duck breasts, and season with 1 teaspoon of salt, 1 teaspoon of pepper, and Espelette pepper.

3. Heat a nonstick skillet on high heat. Place the breasts in it, fat-side down. Cook for 2 minutes. Lower the heat to medium. Drain the potatoes, pat them dry, and add them to the skillet. After 10 minutes of cooking, flip the duck breasts, and cook for one last minute. Place the duck breasts on a serving dish and cover.

4. Flip the potatoes. Brown them for 2 to 3 minutes, then flip again. After 10 minutes, add the garlic, parsley, remaining teaspoon of salt, and remaining teaspoon of pepper. Serve immediately.

Pairing: Pair with a full-bodied red wine, such as Bordeaux.

CHAPON FARCI

STUFFED CAPON WITH CHESTNUTS

Prep time: 15 minutes, plus 1 hour for seasoning ✦ *Cook time: 3 hours*

CLASSIC

1 (6-pound) capon

2 slices of stale bread

⅓ cup milk

7 ounces ground veal

3 ounces sausage meat

2 tablespoons minced
fresh parsley

1 egg

3 shallots, medium
size, minced

1 teaspoon salt

2 teaspoon freshly
ground pepper

4 garlic cloves, divided

1 cup water

1 pound chestnuts

SERVES 4 · A smaller bird, the capon is a beautiful meat that is almost always on the menu during the holidays, because of its great taste. This capon stuffed with chestnuts is the perfect poultry dish for Christmas or New Year's Eve.

1. Take the capon out of the fridge an hour before cooking, and sprinkle salt all over.

2. Soak the stale bread in the milk in a medium bowl.

3. In the bowl of a food processor, mix the ground veal with the bread. Add the sausage meat, parsley, egg, shallots, salt, and pepper. Peal and dice a clove of garlic, and add to the mixture. Process until the mixture seems homogenous.

4. Place the stuffing in the cavity of the bird, then truss it. Place the capon in a roasting pan. Pour ¼ cup water in the bottom, and add the 3 remaining unpeeled garlic cloves. Put the capon in a cold oven, and set the heat at 400°F. With a tablespoon, regularly sprinkle the capon with the cooking juices. Cook for 3 hours, adding more water as it evaporates.

5. Thirty minutes before the end of the cooking time, add the chestnuts to the bottom of the dish. Serve in the roasting pan.

DINDE DE NOËL

CHRISTMAS TURKEY

Prep time: 20 minutes ✦ Cook time: 3 to 4 hours

CLASSIC

1 turkey

2 teaspoons salt, divided

2 teaspoons freshly ground
pepper, divided

1 small black truffle, divided

¼ cup milk

4 slices stale bread

2 medium onions, minced

3 tablespoons minced
fresh parsley

3 ounces ground veal

3 ounces sausage meat

1 egg

¼ cup cognac

2 pounds small potatoes

SERVES 6 · Like in the United States, turkey is also a holiday bird in France, but of course, it's not eaten in November: There were no pilgrims in France, and therefore, no Thanksgiving! However, Christmas turkey is a great tradition. It's usually cooked with chestnuts (just like the capon recipe) or with black truffles.

1. Take the heart, liver, and gizzard out of the turkey and sprinkle 1 teaspoon of salt and 1 teaspoon of pepper inside the cavity and on the skin.

2. Cut the truffle in very thin slices. Reserve a teaspoon for the stuffing. Put the rest of the slices under the skin of the turkey.

3. Preheat the oven to 350°F.

4. Fill a medium bowl with milk and soak the stale slices of bread in it. In the bowl of a food processor, mix the bread with the onions, parsley, and the turkey's liver, heart, and gizzard. Process until smooth. Add the veal and sausage meat, egg, and cognac, process until smooth. Stuff the turkey and truss it.

5. Pour ½ inch of water in a roasting pan and place the turkey in it. Roast the turkey for 18 minutes per pound.

6. Thirty minutes before serving, add the potatoes in their skin to the bottom of the pan.

7. Take out the potatoes and place them on a serving dish. Place the turkey on a platter, carve, and serve.

MEAT

CHAPTER THIRTEEN

THE FRENCH LOVE THEIR MEAT. And, as much as I would love to be able to say that it is, I must confess that my country is not very vegetarian friendly. It's not that we don't love vegetables. It's that we like to taste everything, and meat has amazing flavors and textures. That's why we eat (almost) anything, from pigeon to hedgehog (a traditional meat among the Romani people who've lived in France for centuries). I myself was raised eating horse meat (there was only one butcher in my village and he only sold horse) and a lot of offal (heart, liver, tripe, tongue), which is to me a great way to respect the animal that gave its life for you to survive: You eat every part you can.

La viande—meat—is the most common *plat principal*—main course—on a French menu. I tried here to choose a nice selection of typical dishes that you can easily make in the United States. Because beef and pork cuts are different in the two countries, it takes a little adaptation, but it is worth the effort. Try and go to a "real" butcher as much as you can, and buy organic, grass-fed, "happy" meat. It can cost more, but it makes all the difference to the ecosystem, in your body, and on your palate. And as the French often say, less is more: It's okay to have meat less often if you only have the best.

STEAK TARTARE

Prep time: 5 minutes ✦ *Cook time: It's raw!*

Origin: Paris

DAIRY FREE · GLUTEN FREE · UNDER 30 MINUTES · CLASSIC

FOR THE STEAK TARTARE

1½ pounds trimmed
center-cut beef tenderloin

6 green onions, minced

3 tablespoons chopped
fresh parsley

2 tablespoons cornichons

4 eggs, very fresh

2 tablespoons capers,
drained

FOR SERVING

Dijon mustard

Ketchup

Worcestershire sauce

Tabasco sauce

Olive oil

Salt

Freshly ground pepper

SERVES 4 · Another classic on a Parisian bistro menu, this recipe requires even less cooking than Steak Frites (page 176)—there's none! Steak Tartare is a steak served raw, with accoutrements (like Frites [page 136], of course). Each guest can then proceed to make their own steak, where they can mix spices, egg, and herbs.

1. Grind the meat or chop it yourself with a butcher knife (it's then called *Tartare au couteau*). Shape into 4 patties and place on a serving dish.

2. Put the onions in a serving bowl. Place the parsley in another serving bowl.

3. Drain the cornichons and cut them in thin slices. Break the eggs cautiously—reserve the whites for another recipe. Leave the yolk in half a shell. Place the egg in its shell next to the beef patty, and add a full teaspoon of capers and a full teaspoon of cornichons to the plate.

4. Serve immediately with the bowls of onions and parsley, and with Dijon mustard, ketchup, Worcestershire sauce, Tabasco sauce, olive oil, salt, and pepper on the table.

Le Petit Truc Get the freshest meat you can and eat it the same day. Tell your butcher you are going to make a tartare with it so they give you the freshest they have.

Pairing: Pair with a young dry red wine (one that hasn't aged too much), like a Bourgogne or Beaujolais, or a pinot noir.

STEAK FRITES

Prep time: 5 minutes, plus 45 minutes for marinating ✦ *Cook time: 2 minutes*

GLUTEN FREE · CLASSIC

¼ cup cognac or brandy,
plus 1 tablespoon

4 (½-pound) steak filets,
about 1 inch thick

4 tablespoons crushed
black peppercorns

2 tablespoons butter

1 teaspoon salt

⅔ cup crème fraîche
or whipping cream

2 pounds Frites (page 136)

SERVES 4 · The number one French favorite on their top-ten list of best dishes ever, Steak Frites is nevertheless as simple as its name: it's just steak and Frites (page 136)! But it has to be the best steak with the best Frites and, if possible, the best sauce, too! Here is a recipe with a *sauce au poivre,* a peppercorn sauce that adds even more flavor and pleasure to the mix.

1. Pour 4 tablespoons of cognac in a large dish, place the steaks in it, flip, and marinate for 30 minutes at room temperature.

2. Pour the crushed peppercorns onto a plate, press the meat into the peppers so that they stick. Flip the steak to coat both sides in the pepper. Let rest for 15 minutes.

3. In a large nonstick pan, melt the butter over high heat, and add the steaks. Cook for 2 minutes on each side, then sprinkle with salt. Place the steaks on serving plates and reserve.

4. Pour remaining tablespoon cognac and the cream into the pan. Use a wooden spatula to stir well and bring to a boil. When the cream starts bubbling, stir well and pour the sauce gently onto the steaks.

5. Serve with Frites.

Le Petit Truc French and American butchers don't cut beef the same way, which means it can be tricky to get the exact same part of the animal you would have in Paris. Ask for a flat iron, rib eye, or filet mignon. Make sure it's not too thick.

Pairing: Pair with a full-bodied red wine, such as Bordeaux.

TOURNEDOS ROSSINI

TOURNEDOS, FOIE GRAS, AND BLACK TRUFFLE

Prep time: 5 minutes ✦ Cook time: 5 minutes

Origin: Paris

GLUTEN FREE · UNDER 30 MINUTES · CLASSIC

4 (6-ounce) tournedos
or 2-inch-thick filets mignon

1 teaspoon salt

1 teaspoon freshly
ground pepper

2 tablespoons butter

4 thick slices of stale bread

¼ cup cognac or brandy

4 slices of foie gras,
¼ inch thick and 2 inches
in diameter

1 small (½-ounce) fresh
black truffle, sliced

SERVES 4 · This over-the-top meat recipe combines three deluxe ingredients: foie gras, beef filet, and black truffle. Tournedos Rossini was invented in the ninteenth century for the famous and very gourmet opera composer Gioachino Rossini. Here is a modernized version that enhances the flavors.

1. Take the meat out of the fridge 30 minutes before serving. Season with salt and pepper on each side, and reserve.

2. Melt the butter in a nonstick skillet on medium heat. Gently brown the slices of bread, flipping often, for around 3 minutes.

3. Take the bread slices out, reserve, and put the meat in the skillet. Increase the heat to high, and cook for 3 to 5 minutes, flipping the filet very often. Pour the cognac, set ablaze (beware of the flames), and take the skillet off the heat.

4. Put a slice of buttered bread on each plate, then put a slice of beef on it. Add a slice of foie gras, then sprinkle with slices of black truffle.

Pairing: Pair with a bottle of full-bodied red wine, preferably an aged Bordeaux (Pomerol or Saint-Émilion) or a malbec.

GIGOT DE SEPT HEURES

SEVEN-HOUR LEG OF LAMB

Prep time: 15 minutes ✦ *Cook time: 7 hours* ✦ *Refrigeration time: 1 hour*

DAIRY FREE · GLUTEN FREE · CLASSIC

1 (about 4 pounds)
lamb leg

4 tablespoons salt

2 tablespoons freshly
ground pepper

10 garlic cloves, divided

4 tablespoons olive oil

1 bouquet garni (see page 13)

6 peppercorns

1 (14.5-ounce) can
diced tomatoes

1 bottle white wine
(sauvignon blanc)

SERVES 8 PEOPLE · This leg of lamb recipe is also called *Gigot à la cuillère*—spoon leg of lamb—because the meat is so tender that you use a spoon, not a knife, to help yourself. Serve with Purée de Pommes de Terre (page 137).

1. An hour before cooking, take the leg of lamb out of the fridge, and rub it with salt and pepper. Cover with a cloth, and reserve.

2. Preheat the oven to 250°F.

3. Clean the lamb leg under fresh water, and pat it dry. Stick 4 garlic peeled cloves in the flesh of the lamb, near the bone.

4. In a large French oven, heat the oil over medium-high heat. Brown the lamb leg on each side for about 4 minutes. Add the 6 remaining unpeeled garlic cloves, bouquet garni, and peppercorns. Pour the diced tomatoes and their juice over the lamb. Then pour the bottle of wine. Cover and put the dish in the oven for 7 hours. Turn it halfway through.

5. Remove the pan from the oven, and use a ladle to take the juices and the tomatoes out of the French oven, and place them in a small saucepan over high heat. The sauce should reduce, and get a brown color.

6. Pour the sauce over the lamb and serve.

Pairing: Pair with a nice bottle of tannic red wine, such as Gigondas or Chateauneuf du Pape.

CÔTES DE PORC À LA MOUTARDE

DIJON MUSTARD PORK CHOPS

Prep time: 5 minutes ✦ Cook time: 35 minutes

Origin: Burgundy

GLUTEN FREE

½ cup (1 stick) butter

1 pound potatoes,
peeled, halved

¼ cup crème fraîche
or whipped cream

8 tablespoons Dijon mustard

1 teaspoon salt

1 teaspoon freshly
ground pepper

4 pork chops

SERVES 4 · Pork chops in Dijon mustard are great, and they are even better with potatoes cooked in the same pot! Here is my friend Vincent's grandmother's recipe! I love how it is all made in the same pot, the traditional *cocotte minute*—the pressure cooker. I love how simple it is to make, how tender the meat is, and how delicious the potatoes are!

1. Melt the butter in the pressure cooker over medium heat.

2. Place the halved potatoes in the pressure cooker.

3. In a medium bowl, combine the crème fraîche with the Dijon mustard, stir well, add salt and pepper, and spread on the pork chops.

4. Place the pork chops on the potatoes, cover, close the pressure cooker, and cook for 30 minutes.

5. Serve the confit potatoes and the pork immediately, with a bottle of Dijon mustard.

Le Petit Truc You can also substitute apples for the potatoes for a sweet and sour dish.

Pairing: Pair with a young red wine (one that hasn't aged too much), such as pinot noir.

ESCALOPES DE VEAU À LA NORMANDE

VEAL SCALOPPINI IN CREAM

Prep time: 5 minutes ✦ Cook time: 30 minutes

Origin: Normandy

GLUTEN FREE · UNDER 30 MINUTES

2 tablespoons butter

1 minced onion

4 (8-ounce) veal scaloppini

½ pound button mushrooms, trimmed at the feet, then quartered

1 cup cider

1 cup crème fraîche, or sour cream

1 teaspoon salt

1 teaspoon freshly ground pepper

SERVES 4 · Veal is a very popular meat in France, and a favorite of kids because of its mild flavors. These *escalopes* cooked in cream and cider are named after the Normandy region, where most of the main ingredients come from: good veal, good butter, good crème fraîche . . . and good cider! You can also make this recipe with chicken or turkey breast pounded very thin. Serve with cider, nonalcoholic for the kids!

1. Melt the butter in a nonstick skillet over medium heat. Add the onion, stir well and cook for 5 minutes. Reduce the heat to low, and put the veal scaloppini in the skillet. Cook for 5 minutes on each side. Then use a wooden spatula to take them out of the skillet, put them on a plate, wrap with aluminum foil, and reserve.

2. Put the skillet back on the burner, over medium heat, and add the mushrooms. Cook them slowly for 5 minutes, stirring well: the water from the mushrooms should evaporate, and the mushrooms get slightly brown. When the mushrooms are done, pour in the cider and lower the heat to a simmer. When the sauce has reduced by half, add the cream, salt, and pepper. Stir well. Return the scaloppini back to the skillet for 1 minute.

Le Petit Truc Serve warm, with steamed French beans or small boiled potatoes.

Pairing: Pair with cider.

SAUCISSES AU CHOU

SAUSAGE WITH CABBAGE

Prep time: 10 minutes ✦ *Cook time 75 minutes*

DAIRY FREE · GLUTEN FREE

1 cabbage

1 tablespoon baking soda

½ pound bacon, cut into
½-inch-wide sticks

8 (4-ounce) pork sausages

1 teaspoon salt

1 teaspoon freshly
ground pepper

SERVES 4 · Maybe the easiest and fastest recipe I make in winter and a favorite of the whole family. My mom taught me how to make this simple and delicious meal that takes a wink to prepare and never fails! I usually use mild Italian sausages or kielbasa.

1. Wash the cabbage, core it, and discard the outer leaves. Fill a large saucepan with water, and bring to a boil over high heat. Add the baking soda and blanch the cabbage leaves in it for 5 minutes (see page 19, for more on blanching). Then use a colander to drain, separate the leaves, and set the cabbage aside.

2. Heat a French oven or any cast-iron pot over medium-high heat, and cook the bacon for 2 minutes, stirring often with a wooden spoon. Using a fork, prick the sausages, then add them to the pot and brown them on each side, for about 5 minutes.

3. Add the cabbage leaves to the pot, stir well, then reduce the heat to low. Add salt and pepper, and cover the pot. Simmer for an hour.

Le Petit Truc You can actually use any cabbage for this recipe. From kale to napa cabbage to red cabbage (the latter gives a nice purple color to the whole dish!). I also sometimes add boiled potatoes as a side dish.

Pairing: Pair with a nice beer.

LAPIN À LA MOUTARDE

MUSTARD RABBIT STEW

Prep time: 15 minutes ✦ Cook time: 60 minutes

GLUTEN FREE

2 tablespoons butter

3 shallots, finely sliced

1 rabbit, head removed, cut into chunks

4 tablespoons Dijon mustard

1 tablespoon rosemary (preferably a sprig)

1 teaspoon salt

1 teaspoon freshly ground pepper

1 cup white wine

½ cup crème fraîche or Mexican crema

SERVES 4 · Rabbit is also quite a common meat in French cuisine—my grandmothers always had some in the backyard. It's a lean and healthy meat—full of calcium and phosphorus, it's recommended for people who have high cholesterol. It's also full of flavor and is delicious when cooked with Dijon mustard.

1. In a French oven or cast-iron pot, melt the butter over medium heat. Add the shallots, cook for 2 minutes, then add the rabbit parts and brown on all sides. Cook for 5 minutes, then reduce the heat to low. Add the Dijon mustard, rosemary, salt, and pepper. Stir well. Cover the pot and simmer for 10 minutes.

2. Add the white wine and cream, and stir well. Cover again and cook slowly for 45 minutes.

Le Petit Truc Serve warm with pasta or steamed French beans.

Pairing: Pair with white wine, preferably from Burgundy.

HACHIS PARMENTIER

SHEPHERD'S PIE

Prep time: 15 minutes ✦ Cook time: 90 minutes

GLUTEN FREE

1 tablespoon salt,
plus 1 teaspoon

2 pounds potatoes, peeled

1 tablespoon olive oil

1 onion, minced

1½ pounds braised beef

1 cup beef stock

2 ounces butter, diced,
at room temperature

1½ cup whole milk

1 teaspoon freshly
ground pepper

2 ounces grated cheese
(Gruyère is better, but
mozzarella is okay)

SERVES 4 · This French version of Shepherd's Pie is a very traditional family dish, and also the best way to recycle Boeuf Bourguignon (page 90) leftovers!

1. Fill a large saucepan with water, add a tablespoon of salt, and boil the potatoes for 20 minutes.

2. Heat the olive oil in a nonstick skillet, over medium heat, then cook the onions for 2 minutes, stirring well. Shred the braised meat, add to the pot, and pour in the beef stock. Stir well, and cook for 15 minutes over low heat.

3. Preheat the oven to 350°F.

4. When the potatoes are boiled, drain them and mash them in a bowl. Add the butter, then pour the milk in slowly, stirring steadily until you get a smooth texture. Add the remaining teaspoon of salt and the pepper, and stir again.

5. Spread half of the mashed potatoes in a large casserole dish. Then spread the meat on top. Finally spread the rest of the mashed potatoes on the meat. Sprinkle grated cheese all over, and cook for 45 minutes.

Le Petit Truc If you don't have already-braised beef, sauté 1 minced onion in butter with 1 pound of ground beef, 2 minced tomatoes, and a garlic clove. Add ½ cup of beef stock, season with a teaspoon of salt and pepper, cook for 5 minutes. Then add to the recipe.

Pairing: Pair with red wine, like Beaujolais.

TOMATES FARCIES

STUFFED TOMATOES

Prep time: 15 minutes ✦ *Cook time: 45 minutes*

8 large tomatoes

1 tablespoon salt, plus 1 teaspoon

1 cup whole milk

2 slices stale bread

2 medium-size shallots, minced

2 tablespoons minced fresh parsley

2 tablespoons thyme

1 pound sausage meat

½ pound ground veal

1 teaspoon freshly ground pepper

½ cup rice

1 cup water

SERVES 4 · Always a hit with kids, and a great family dinner, stuffed tomatoes are the best summer one-pot meal! You can also stuff the tomatoes with zucchini, onions, or potatoes.

1. Cut away the top of each tomato, at about ½ inch from the top: The French call it the *chapeau*—the hat. Reserve. With a spoon, scoop out the tomatoes, removing the seeds and the innards. Reserve the innards of the tomatoes in a separate bowl. Sprinkle a tablespoon of salt inside each tomato.

2. Preheat the oven to 350°F.

3. Pour the milk into a soup plate, and soak the bread slices in it. Then cut them into very small pieces, or process in a blender.

4. In the bowl of a food processor, mix the shallots, bread, parsley, and thyme. Pour in a large bowl, add the sausage meat and the veal, mix with a fork, add remaining teaspoon of salt and the pepper, and mix again. Stuff mixture into each tomato. Cover each with a "tomato hat."

5. Pour the tomatoes' innards in the bottom of a large baking dish Add the rice. Pour 1 of cup water over the rice and tomatoes.

6. Place the tomatoes in the dish, over the rice. Put in the oven and cook for 45 minutes.

7. The rice will cook and soak up the tomato juice. Serve warm.

Pairing: Pair with a nice bottle of chilled rosé, a Touraine rosé for instance.

TARTES AND "PETITS GÂTEAUX"

CHAPTER FOURTEEN

THE STRUGGLE IS REAL. I must confess it has been especially hard to pick the recipes for these last two chapters. There are so many amazing French sweet recipes to choose from! At the end, there must be a reason why my people invented the word "dessert."

So I decided to split them into two chapters. This one is all about Tartes and Petits Gâteaux—pies and cookies—two fabulous types of sweets that play a great part in one of my favorite meals: *le goûter.* Or, as French kids say *"le 4 heures,"* because it usually takes place at 4 p.m., sharp! For little ones but also for adults, with tea, coffee, *chocolat chaud,* or a chilled bottle of champagne, these recipes are just perfect!

I myself am a big fan of *tartes,* and really love how the French sweet pies are always all about the fruits. As often in French cuisine, it's about simple, straightforward tastes, and about trying to find the best way to showcase the main fresh ingredients. Find the best apples, strawberries, or lemon, and make the best of it!

Petits gateaux are also great, and perfect to snack or nibble. In France you don't keep them in cookie jars, but in metallic airtight boxes that preserve the flavors and textures better.

TARTE TATIN

APPLE UPSIDE-DOWN TART

Prep time: 15 minutes ✦ *Cook time: 45 minutes*

Origin: Loire Valley

VEGETARIAN · CLASSIC

1¼ cups brown sugar, divided

3 tablespoons water

3 pounds apples, peeled and cored

3 tablespoons butter, diced

1 Pâte Brisée (page 27)

SERVES 6 · This upside-down apple pie was invented by two sisters who owned a small restaurant in the Loire Valley. One was so stressed out that she baked the pie upside down without noticing. The customers loved it, and the rest is history!

1. Preheat the oven to 425°F.

2. In a small saucepan, mix ¾ cup of sugar and 3 tablespoons of water. Bring slowly to a boil over moderate heat. As soon as the sugar gets golden, pour the caramel in a 12-inch pie plate. Tilt to let the caramel spread everywhere.

3. Cut the apples in big slices, about ½ inch thick, and place them over the caramel. Sprinkle remaining ½ cup of sugar on them, and place the butter on top.

4. Roll the dough out into a 13-inch round, and place it on top of the apples. Using a knife, cut off the dough that is more than 1 inch out of the pan. Tuck it in around the edges of the pan.

5. Put in the oven for 10 minutes at 425°F, then reduce the heat to 400°F and cook for another 30 minutes. As soon as you take it out of the oven, put a large plate on the pie, and turn it over. The crust will be on the bottom and the caramelized apples on top.

Pairing: Pair with a glass of cider, champagne, or tea and *chocolat chaud.*

TARTE AUX POMMES

FRENCH APPLE PIE

Prep time: 15 minutes ✦ *Cook time: 45 minutes*

Origin : Normandy

VEGETARIAN · CLASSIC

1 Pâte Brisée (page 27)

½ cup applesauce

2 pounds apples, cored and
cut into thin slices

2 tablespoons brown sugar

1 tablespoon butter, diced

SERVES 6 · Just a simple butter crust, apples, and sugar. Nothing is as French as Tarte aux Pommes! French apple pie is as easy to make as it is to eat—above all if you use ready-made apple-sauce. Serve with cider or champagne or à la mode. Although à la mode is not that French: it's very rare to serve pie with ice cream in France!

1. Preheat your oven to 350°F.

2. Roll out the crust into a 13-inch round, and place it on a sheet of parchment paper. Take a 12-inch pie plate, and put the dough and the parchment paper on it. Fold the dough overhang under, and crimp the edge of the dough. Cut away the parchment paper that is extending out of the plate. Then, with a fork, make small holes all over the pie dough.

3. Spread the applesauce on the bottom, and arrange the apple slices in an overlapping spiral pattern. Sprinkle the sugar and butter on top of the apples. Cook for 45 minutes.

4. Serve warm, lukewarm, or cold!

Le Petit Truc Try to use small apples: they have more flavors and nutrients. Organic apples are even better. Keep the skin on: less work, more taste and vitamins!

Pairing: Pair with cider, champagne, or tea.

TARTE AU CITRON

LEMON PIE

Prep time: 10 minutes ✦ Cook time: 30 minutes

VEGETARIAN · UNDER 30 MINUTES · CLASSIC

1 cup (2 sticks) butter, divided

2 cups flour

4 eggs

¾ cup brown sugar, divided

5 lemons

SERVES 6 · This lemon pie is everything I love: super easy, super straightforward, and extremely good. It's not a fancy *tarte au citron meringuée* (no meringue in here), but a much simpler and, to my mind, full-of-flavor version. It's all about lemon, and the incredible acidity of citrus.

1. Preheat the oven to 450°F.

2. Melt 1 stick and 1 tablespoon of butter for 30 seconds in the microwave. Pour the flour in a large bowl, create a well in the middle, and break the egg in it. Add ¼ cup of sugar, and the melted butter. Use a wooden spoon to roughly knead the dough for 2 minutes.

3. Rub 1 tablespoon of butter on a 12-inch pie plate. Press the dough with your hands into the plate. Bake for 7 minutes.

4. Grate the lemon zest in a bowl. Juice the lemons. Melt 6 tablespoons of butter in the microwave. In a large bowl, break 3 eggs, whisk in remaining ½ cup of sugar and the butter. Add the lemon juice and the lemon zest, and whisk.

5. Pour the lemon mixture into the prebaked piecrust, and put back in the oven for 10 to 15 minutes.

Le Petit Truc I like using Meyer lemons for a sweeter taste, and you can also try this recipe with 3 oranges or 6 clementines.

Pairing: Pair with champagne or a dry white wine.

TARTE AUX FRAISES

STRAWBERRY AND CREAM PIE

Prep time: 10 minutes, plus 1 hour to cool

VEGETARIAN

1 Pâte Mega-Sablée
(page 29)

1 cup whipping cream

⅓ cup powdered sugar

1 pound strawberries,
halved

SERVES 6 · Fresh strawberries over whipped cream and the best crust ever. I love making this dessert on the spot, right before serving it—just prepare the crust, whip the cream at the last minute, and place the strawberries. It's a perfect birthday cake to my mind. Open a bottle of champagne with it!

1. An hour ahead put the bowl of your stand mixer in the freezer, and your whipping cream in the fridge.

2. Bake the Pâte Mega-Sablée. Let it cool.

3. Right before serving, pour the cream in the bowl of the stand mixer, start whisking slowly, then firmly after 20 seconds. When the cream starts to get thick, add the powdered sugar. Keep whisking until the cream is fluffy.

4. When the crust is cool, spread the whipped cream on the bottom, then arrange the strawberries in a spiral. Serve immediately.

Le Petit Truc You can make this recipe with fresh raspberries.

Pairing: Pair with champagne.

MADELEINES

Prep time: 10 minutes, plus 2 hours to cool ✣ *Cook time: 13 minutes* ✣ *Refrigeration time: 2 hours*

Origin: East of France, Lorraine

VEGETARIAN · UNDER 30 MINUTES · CLASSIC

8 tablespoons butter, divided

2 large eggs

1 egg yolk

½ cup sugar

½ teaspoon baking powder

1 cup flour

MAKES 20 MADELEINES · Marcel Proust, one of the most celebrated French novelists, started his masterpiece *In Search of Lost Time* with the childhood remembrances that suddenly came to his mind when he ate a Madeleine after dipping it in a cup of verbena tea. Now the French say something is their "Madeleine de Proust" when it's the one thing that reminds them of their childhood. A kid's favorite, too! Serve with tea, verbena, or *chocolat chaud!*

1. Melt 7 tablespoons of butter in a small saucepan, over very low heat. Reserve.

2. Preheat the oven to 350°F.

3. In a large bowl, whisk 2 eggs and the egg yolk with the sugar. Add the baking powder, whisking continuously, and add the flour very slowly. Pour in the melted butter, and whisk again until smooth. Cover and put in the fridge for 2 hours.

4. Butter the Madeleine pan if you have the steel version (there is no need to butter a silicone pan), and pour the batter in each cup until it is ¾ full. Cook for 13 minutes.

5. Unmold them as soon as they are out of the oven.

Le Petit Truc Add a teaspoon of matcha powder to the batch and make amazing green tea Madeleines!

Pairing: Pair with champagne or tea.

CANNELÉS

RUM AND VANILLA CAKES

Prep time: 10 minutes ✦ *Cook time: 80 minutes* ✦ *Refrigeration time: 24 hours*

Origin: Bordeaux, Southwest of France

VEGETARIAN · CLASSIC

3 tablespoons butter,
divided

2 cups whole milk

1 vanilla pod, sliced in
half lengthwise

⅔ cup flour

1 cup sugar

2 large eggs, beaten

2 egg yolks

⅔ cup rum

MAKES 20 CANNELÉS · With rum and vanilla flavoring and an incredibly soft texture under their caramelized crust, Cannelés are tiny bits of heaven with only one flaw: the best ones require preparing the batter 24 hours ahead of time. While they are traditionally made in special copper molds, you can now find some silicone models that are much easier to use.

1. In a small saucepan over medium heat, melt 2 tablespoons of butter in the milk. Add the vanilla pod and continue heating until it begins to boil.

2. In a large bowl, whisk the flour and sugar. Add the eggs and the egg yolks. Remove the vanilla from the saucepan, place it on a flat surface, and scrape out the seeds with a paring knife. Add the seeds to the batter and slowly add the milk mixture. Add the rum, whisking well. Wrap and refrigerate for at least 24 hours (for no longer than 48 hours).

3. One hour prior to baking, remove the batter from the refrigerator.

4. Preheat the oven to 500°F. Butter the molds if they are made of metal. Pour the batter into each cup until ¾ full.

5. Bake for 11 minutes, lower the heat to 350°F, and bake for 1 additional hour. Let the cakes cool before removing from the mold.

Pairing: Pair with a white Bordeaux wine.

VRAIS MACARONS

ALMOND COOKIES

Prep time: 10 minutes ✦ *Cook time: 10 minutes*

Origin: Southwest of France

VEGETARIAN · DAIRY FREE · GLUTEN FREE · UNDER 30 MINUTES · CLASSIC

3 egg whites

½ teaspoon salt

1½ cups powdered sugar

1 tablespoon orange
blossom water

1⅓ cups almond flour

MAKES 20 MACARONS · These gluten-free almond cookies are the ancestors to the fancy flavored and colored macarons that are all the rage. I love them, because they are much more straight-forward in taste and flavor, and so easy to make. Plus my gluten-free friends are always so happy to eat them! They were invented in the seventeenth century for a royal wedding and are still made to this day in the best *pâtisseries* of southwestern of France. The family of the inventor actually still makes them and sells them in the family shop in Saint-Jean-de-Luz.

1. Preheat your oven to 350°F.

2. Put the egg whites and the salt in the bowl of a stand mixer. Whisk at moderate speed for 1 minute, then faster, until they are fluffy. Keep whisking and add the sugar, the orange blossom water, and the almond flour. Whisk for another 2 minutes.

3. Place a sheet of parchment paper on a sheet pan. Using a tablespoon, scoop up some of the batter, about the size of a walnut. Roll it with your hands, and press on the parchment paper. The cookies should be about 1¾ inches wide. Let them dry out until you can touch them without your finger getting stuck. Bake for 10 minutes or until the macarons start to become golden.

Pairing: Pair with tea, cider, or champagne.

MERINGUES

Prep time: 15 minutes ✦ *Cook time: 70 minutes*

VEGETARIAN · DAIRY FREE · GLUTEN FREE · CLASSIC

6 egg whites

½ teaspoon salt

½ cup sugar

½ cup powdered sugar

MAKES ABOUT 20 MERINGUES · They are fluffy, white, sweet, delicious, and so easy to make! Meringues are great for tea or *le goûter*, gluten free, and a great way to use the leftover egg whites from all the recipes that only need egg yolks. Try and store the egg whites in an airtight container, and use them after 1 or 2 days—the meringues will be easier to make.

1. Preheat your oven to 200°F.

2. Combine the egg whites and the salt in the bowl of a stand mixer. Whisk at moderate speed, for 1 minute. Add the sugar, tablespoon by tablespoon, increasing the speed of the mixer, until the egg whites are very firm. They should be stiff and shiny.

3. Place a sheet of parchment paper on a sheet pan. Fill a pastry bag with the egg whites, and pipe small round shapes. You can also use two tablespoons to shape them. Sprinkle powdered sugar on them. Put in the oven and cook for 70 minutes. They should dry up, but not get brown.

4. Let them cool before serving.

Pairing: Pair with tea, coffee, chocolate, or even champagne.

BEIGNETS DE MARDI GRAS

CARNIVAL-STYLE DONUTS

Prep time: 20 minutes, plus 2 hours to leaven ✣ Cook time: 20 minutes

Origin: Loire Valley

VEGETARIAN · CLASSIC

3 tablespoons
baker's yeast

2 tablespoons
lukewarm water

4 cups flour

6 tablespoons sugar, divided

3 tablespoons whole milk

4 tablespoons orange
blossom water

4 eggs

⅔ cup butter, cut into small
cubes, at room temperature

Frying oil

MAKES 20 "RONDIAUX" · In France, beignets are traditionally made for Fat Tuesday, the day before the start of Lent, and something like our Halloween: French kids wear costumes and eat tons of sweets!

1. In a small bowl, mix the baker's yeast with the lukewarm water. Cover with a tepid cloth and put it in a warm room for 10 minutes.

2. In a large bowl, mix the flour and 4 tablespoons of sugar. Pour in the milk slowly and stir with a wooden spoon. Add the orange blossom water, eggs, and butter, and knead with your hands for at least 10 minutes, until the butter is totally combined. Cover with a damp cloth, and leave in a warm room for at least 2 hours.

3. On a sheet of parchment paper, roll the dough out until it is ¼ inch thick, and cut it into diamond shapes.

4. Fill a large saucepan with frying oil, bring to medium heat, and fry the beignets. When they are golden on each side, remove them from the oil with a slotted spoon.

5. Sprinkle remaining 2 tablespoon of powdered sugar on top of the beignets.

Pairing: Pair with tea, coffee, chocolate, chicory, cider, or champagne.

PETITS SABLÉS

SHORTBREAD COOKIES

Prep time: 15 minutes ✷ *Cook time: 10 minutes*

VEGETARIAN · UNDER 30 MINUTES · CLASSIC

10 tablespoons butter,
at room temperature

½ cup brown sugar

1 egg

2¼ cups flour

MAKES ABOUT 30 COOKIES · These small cookies are the definition of *petits gateaux.* You should always have a batch ready in case grandkids or friends come over at the last minute! They are also one of the first things French kids learn to make. I remember making them at school.

1. Place the butter in the bowl of a stand mixer, and whisk until very soft, like a face cream. Keep whisking as you add the sugar, egg, and flour. Shape into a ball, wrap and leave in the fridge for 2 hours.

2. Preheat the oven to 350°F.

3. Divide the dough in 2, and place on a sheet of parchment paper, place another sheet on top of the dough, and roll until the dough is ¼-inch thick.

4. Use cookie cutters to cut out as many cookies as you can. Place the cookies on a parchment-lined sheet pan and bake for 10 minutes. They should get slightly brown on the sides. Let them cool.

Le Petit Truc With the tip of a knife, make a hole in each cookie, and use them for Christmas tree decorations with a nice ribbon (my mother-in-law's great idea!).

Pairing: Pair with *chocolat chaud,* hot cocoa, tea, coffee, or cider.

DESSERTS

CHAPTER FIFTEEN

"**L**E MEILLEUR POUR LA FIN . . .**"** Always save the best for last. And how amazing is the end of a meal when a classic French dessert is on the menu. You will find here my favorites to make. Of course *La haute-pâtisserie française,* just like "haute couture," has invented and is still inventing everyday beautiful and very difficult to make sweet miracles. But these beauties are best bought and eaten at one of the upscale *pâtisseries* that flower everywhere in France.

For this book, I tried to choose the homemade desserts, made from scratch from generation to generation, that are so good . . . and so easy to make. Most of them take only a few minutes to prepare, and almost all can be made by a 10-year-old (that's when I learned to make them by myself anyway)! A lot of chocolate, plenty of butter, some crêpes, which are so easy and quick to make at the last minute . . . and two of our great traditional cakes that I miss so much as a French expat: Bûche de Noël (page 219), traditional for Christmas, and Galette des Rois (page 220)—King Cake—one of the most festive and delicious French desserts!

CLAFOUTIS AUX CERISES

CHERRY CAKE

Prep time: 15 minutes ✛ Cook time: 40 minutes

VEGETARIAN · GLUTEN FREE · CLASSIC

6 eggs

⅔ cup brown sugar,
plus 1 tablespoon

½ cup almond flour

¾ cup whipping cream
or Mexican crema

1 tablespoon butter

2 pounds unpitted cherries

2 tablespoons
powdered sugar

SERVES 6 · This iconic French summer cake is a flan-like cake flavored with fresh fruit—usually cherries. This is a gluten-free recipe, which makes the dessert even easier to share with friends. You can replace the cherries with raspberries, plums, or another fruit that is in season. I always keep frozen cherries or raspberries in the freezer so I can make a last-minute dessert. Just add them to the baking dish; no need to thaw.

1. Preheat the oven to 400°F.

2. In a large bowl, break the eggs and whisk with ⅔ cup of brown sugar for 2 minutes or until the custard whitens. Add the almond flour, whisking continuously. Slowly add the whipping cream and whisk until homogeneous.

3. Butter a medium baking dish. Sprinkle 1 tablespoon of sugar on the bottom and tilt the dish to spread out the sugar. Place the cherries at the bottom of the dish and pour in the custard.

4. Bake for 40 minutes and sift a bit of powdered sugar on top. Let it cool.

Le Petit Truc The traditional recipe calls for unpitted cherries, but the pits give more flavor. Of course, use pitted fruits if kids are going to eat the cake.

Pairing: Pair with a good lemonade, champagne, or a sweet white wine.

GÂTEAU AU YAOURT

YOGURT CAKE

Prep time: 15 minutes ✦ *Cook time: 25 minutes*

VEGETARIAN · CLASSIC

1 yogurt cup (⅔ cup) plain whole-milk yogurt

3 eggs

1 yogurt cup (⅔ cup) canola or olive oil

2 yogurt cups (1⅓ cups) sugar

3 yogurt cups (2 cups) flour

2 tablespoons baking powder

¼ teaspoon salt

1 teaspoon orange blossom water

1 tablespoon butter

SERVES 6 · This is the first cake a French kid learns to make, and it is always a success! Yogurt cake measurements are based on the yogurt, and a yogurt cup should be used to measure everything. You can buy a glass yogurt cup, use a regular cup of yogurt from the store, or use the measurements I found. This cake is always beautiful and nice, it can be a great base for a birthday cake (add glaze, or fresh strawberries and whipped cream on top), or you can add sliced apples or other fruits in it.

1. Preheat the oven to 340°F.

2. In a large bowl, whisk the yogurt with the eggs. Add the oil, sugar, flour, orange blossom water, baking powder, and salt, and whisk until you get a homogeneous mixture.

3. Butter a round 8-inch baking dish and pour in the batter.

4. Bake for 25 minutes.

Le Petit Truc You can also grate the peel of a lime in the batter for more taste, or a tablespoon of grated ginger.

GÂTEAU DE SAVOIE

GLUTEN-FREE SPONGE CAKE

Prep time: 15 minutes �֍ Cook time: 45 minutes

Origin: Savoie, the Alps

VEGETARIAN · GLUTEN FREE · CLASSIC

6 eggs, whites and yolks
separated

¼ teaspoon salt

¾ cup sugar, divided

1 egg yolk

1 lemon

1⅛ cups cornstarch

1 tablespoon butter

SERVES 6 · This delicious sponge cake used to be my mom's worst nightmare. Her own mom loved to serve Gâteau de Savoie, and she always asked her to whip the egg whites to help make the cake—but at the time, they had no electrical whip, so the process was very tiring. These days, everything is much easier, and you can enjoy this light cake that is great served with fresh berries, and that is also gluten-free!

1. Preheat the oven to 425°F.

2. In the bowl of a stand mixer, whisk the egg whites and the salt at moderate speed for 1 minute. Speed it up and add ¼ cup of sugar. Whisk until very firm.

3. Use another bowl to whisk the 7 egg yolks. Keep whisking as you add the remaining ½ cup of sugar. Zest the lemon very finely over the bowl. Whisk for 10 minutes.

4. Slowly fold 1 tablespoon of egg white mixture and 1 tablespoon of cornstarch to the egg yolk mixture. Repeat until all cornstarch and egg whites have been incorporated.

5. Butter a 9-inch dish. Pour in the batter and bake for 5 minutes. Lower the heat to 250°F and bake for another 40 minutes. Let it cool down before serving.

FONDANT AU CHOCOLAT

ALMOST-FLOURLESS CHOCOLATE CAKE

Prep time: 10 minutes ✦ *Cook time: 25 minutes*

VEGETARIAN · CLASSIC

11 tablespoons butter, divided

1¼ cups dark chocolate chips, 60% cocoa minimum

3 large eggs

¾ cup sugar

½ cup flour

SERVES 6 · Because any good French cook has a good chocolate cake recipe, and also because it is of course always a crowd pleaser. I love making chocolate cake, it's been a hobby with my brother since I was 10. This recipe is easy to make with kids, unless they eat the whole bowl of chocolate before you even put it in the oven! Serve with some whipped cream, or à la mode.

1. Preheat the oven to 350°F.

2. Melt 10 tablespoons of butter with the chocolate in a small saucepan, over low heat. Using a wooden spoon, stir until smooth, remove from the heat and let it cool down.

3. In a large bowl, whisk the eggs, add the sugar, then add the melted chocolate and butter. Add the flour slowly, and whisk until smooth.

4. Butter a 9-inch round springform pan. Pour the mixture in it. Bake for 25 minutes.

Le Petit Truc I like adding a teaspoon of Espelette or cayenne pepper to spice up the cake. For a last-minute glaze, you can spread 2 tablespoons of apricot jam all over the cake.

Pairing: Pair with a nice bottle of tannic red wine or a glass of brandy.

PROFITEROLES AU CHOCOLAT

CHOCOLATE AND ICE CREAM PUFFS

Prep time: 20 minutes · Cook time: 20 minutes

VEGETARIAN · CLASSIC

⅓ cup water

¼ cup whole milk

⅓ cup butter, diced at room temperature

½ teaspoon salt

1 teaspoon sugar

¾ cup flour

3 large eggs

⅓ cup whipping cream

1 cup dark chocolate chips

1 cup Crème Chantilly (page 31)

SERVES 4 · A great choice on any good dessert menu, Profiteroles make a dramatic dessert and please any sweet tooth.

1. Preheat the oven to 400°F.

2. In a medium saucepan over medium heat, combine the water, milk, butter, salt, and sugar. Stir with a wooden spoon. When the mixture starts to boil, remove from the heat. Pour in the flour, stirring until it doesn't stick to the bottom. Return the saucepan to the stove and continue stirring over low heat for 2 minutes. Pour the mixture in a large bowl. Add the eggs, one by one. Stir until homogenous.

3. Place a sheet of parchment paper over a sheet pan. Using a pastry bag, or just two teaspoons, shape small mounds of dough (about 1 inch wide) on the parchment paper. Bake for 10 minutes, then lower the oven to 350°F and bake for another 10 minutes.

4. In a small saucepan, bring the whipping cream to a boil over medium heat. Add the chocolate, lower the heat, and stir until melted.

5. Cut each puff ⅓ of the way down. Using a pastry bag or a teaspoon, fill the inside with Crème Chantilly, and put the top back on. Pour chocolate sauce on each puff and serve immediately.

Le Petit Truc You can also fill the Profiteroles with vanilla ice cream. Pour the hot chocolate sauce on the top at the last minute.

Pairing: Pair with a sweet white wine.

POTS DE CRÈME AU CHOCOLAT

CHOCOLATE POTS DE CRÈME

Prep time: 15 minutes ✦ *Cook time: 30 minutes* ✦ *Refrigeration time: 30 minutes*

VEGETARIAN · GLUTEN FREE · CLASSIC

2 cups whole milk

5 egg yolks

⅓ cup sugar

½ pound dark
chocolate chips

SERVES 8 · A nice treat at the end of the meal, these small chocolate custard ramekins make a lighter dessert, with an always appreciated touch of chocolate. Did I mention kids just love them?

1. Pour ½ to 1 inch of cold water into a large baking dish and preheat the oven to 300°F.

2. Pour the milk in a large saucepan, and warm it over medium heat. Remove from the heat right before it boils.

3. In the bowl of a stand mixer, whisk the egg yolks and the sugar until the mixture whitens. Pour in ⅓ of the warm milk, keep whisking for 2 minutes. Then pour the egg mixture back into the saucepan, with the rest of the warm milk.

4. Place the egg and milk mixture over low heat and add the chocolate chips, stirring continuously until melted and fluid. Pour into ramekins, place them in the prepared baking dish, and cook for 30 minutes.

5. Let the ramekins cool down at room temperature and refrigerate them for 2 hours before serving.

Pairing: Pair with a bottle of Bordeaux.

MOUSSE AU CHOCOLAT

CHOCOLATE MOUSSE

Prep time: 15 minutes ✦ *Refrigeration time: 4 hours*

VEGETARIAN · GLUTEN FREE · CLASSIC

1½ cups dark chocolate chips (preferably more than 66% cocoa)

6 large eggs, whites and yolks separated

¼ teaspoon salt

SERVES 4 · It's airy, it's full of chocolate, it's our inner-child's dream. Chocolate mousse is the best! Serve with fresh berries or pears, and a tannic red wine, or champagne. You can also spice it up by adding a tablespoon of black coffee to the chocolate (this is how my mom does it anyway).

1. Fill a large saucepan with water, place over moderate heat, and place a smaller saucepan on top. Add the chocolate and melt it slowly.

2. Put the egg whites and the salt in the bowl of a stand mixer. Whisk moderately for the first minute, then increase the speed as the whites get firmer. Stop when the whites are extra firm.

3. In a large bowl, whisk the chocolate with the egg yolks.

4. Add the egg whites tablespoon by tablespoon to the chocolate mixture. Fold them into the chocolate, using a wooden spoon, until combined. Cover with plastic wrap and put in the fridge for at least 4 hours.

Le Petit Truc My mom always melts ¼ cup of white chocolate, too, that she incorporates with 4 tablespoons of the whipped egg whites, and pours in the middle of the black chocolate mousse.

Pairing: Pair with a tannic red wine or champagne.

MILLEFEUILLE

NAPOLEONS

Prep time: 20 minutes ✦ *Cook time: 22 minutes*

VEGETARIAN · CLASSIC

2 puff pastry sheets

2 tablespoons brown sugar, plus ⅓ cup

⅓ cup powdered sugar

1⅓ cups whole milk

2 eggs

⅓ cup flour

1 tablespoon orange blossom water or vanilla extract

SERVES 6 · You might know this cake under the name of Napoleon, although the tiny but powerful French emperor is not linked to this dessert at all in France, where it is more poetically called Millefeuille—thousand layers. A classic French dessert made with two classic French pastry ingredients: puff pastry and *crème patissière*.

1. Roll out the pastry sheets, and cut them into 6 (3-by-8-inch) rectangles. Put them in the fridge for ½ hour.

2. Preheat your oven to 450°F.

3. Cover a sheet pan with parchment paper and place the pastry sheet rectangles on top. Sprinkle 2 tablespoons of brown sugar on them, and place a second sheet pan on top, to prevent from rising too much. Put in the oven, lower the heat to 375°F. After 7 minutes, remove the top sheet pan, cover with parchment paper, and bake for another 10 minutes.

4. Take out of the oven, sprinkle powdered sugar all over, and bake for another 5 minutes. Take out of the oven and cool down.

5. Prepare the *crème patissière:* Bring the milk to a boil in a small saucepan. In the bowl of a stand mixer, whisk the eggs and the remaining ⅓ cup of brown sugar. Add the flour and keep whisking as you slowly pour the warm milk over the egg mixture. Return mixture to the saucepan, over very low heat. Whisk for 15 minutes, stop as soon as the first bubbles appear. Pour the orange blossom water into the saucepan, and reserve.

6. Cut (very carefully) each cooked pastry rectangle into 3 equal pieces. Lay the first piece on a serving plate. Spread a nice layer of cream. Add a piece of puffed pastry, spread cream on it, and top with a last piece of puff pastry. Repeat for the 5 other servings and sprinkle powdered sugar on top of them all.

Le Petit Truc You can also fill the Millefeuille with a mix of ½ *crème patissière* and ½ Crème Chantilly (page 31).

CRÊPES SUCRÉES

SWEET CRÊPES

Prep time: 10 minutes ✣ *Cook time: 15 minutes*

Origin: Normandy

VEGETARIAN · UNDER 30 MINUTES

FOR THE CRÊPES

1 tablespoon butter

1 batch Pâte à Crêpes
(page 32)

FOR THE CHOCOLATE

1 cup chocolate chips

¼ cup whipping cream

SERVES 6 · There's nothing like a crêpes party for dessert or *le goûter,* the 4 p.m. snack. Cheap, quick, and easy, everybody loves them. Just prepare a nice batter, get the crêpe pan going, and set up all the accouterments your guests might like on the table. Crêpes with jam, honey, chocolate, Créme Chantilly (page 31), or plain sugar? Let your guests decide!

TO MAKE THE CRÊPES

1. In a medium nonstick skillet (preferably a crêpe pan), melt 1 teaspoon of the butter over medium-high heat. Wipe it out with a paper cloth. Then take a small ladleful of batter, pour it in the center of the pan, and immediately swirl the pan so that the batter spreads all over. Cook until the rim of the crêpe detaches itself from the pan, then use a wooden spatula to flip it onto the other side. Cook for about 1 minute.

2. Pile up the crêpes on a large plate, cover with aluminum foil, and place the plate on a small saucepan filled with water, over low heat. This will make sure they stay warm.

Fill half of a large saucepan with water, bring to a boil, and place a smaller saucepan with the chocolate and the whipping cream on top. Stir until melted. Pour into a serving bowl.

FOR SERVING

Serve all crêpes with a bowl of Crème Chantilly (page 31), sugar, melted chocolate, honey, and jam on the table, and invite your guests to choose the filling they prefer.

Le Petit Truc The French always celebrate crêpes on February 2nd for *la Chandeleur.* You're supposed to cook your crêpes with a coin in your left hand. If you manage to flip it with just one hand, you will have money all year long!

Pairing: Pair with cider or champagne.

CRÊPES SUZETTE

Prep time: 15 minutes ✣ Cook time: 15 minutes ✣ Refrigeration time: 1 hour

VEGETARIAN · UNDER 30 MINUTES · CLASSIC

Origin: Paris

FOR THE CRÊPES

1 tablespoon butter, divided

1 batch Pâte à Crêpes
(page 32)

FOR THE FILLING

3 mandarin oranges,
reserve peel

⅓ cup butter, cut into small
cubes, at room temperature,
plus 1 tablespoon

⅓ cup sugar

½ cup plus 2 tablespoons
Grand Marnier or triple sec,
divided

SERVES 4 · It's always so dramatic to see flames in a restaurant! When a French waiter sets a pan ablaze in front of all the customers, it is of course to serve Crêpes Suzette. This recipe is now considered vintage and somewhat outdated, but some French people are fighting for it to make a comeback. It's so good, too!

TO MAKE THE CRÊPES

1. In a medium nonstick skillet (preferably a crêpe pan), melt 1 teaspoon of the butter over medium-high heat. Wipe it out with a paper cloth. Then take a small ladleful of batter, pour it in the center of the pan, and immediately swirl the pan so that the batter spreads all over. Cook until the rim of the crêpe detaches itself from the pan, then use a wooden spatula to flip it. Cook for about 1 minute.

2. Pile up the crêpes on a large plate, cover with aluminum foil, and place the plate on top of a small saucepan filled with water over low heat. This will make sure they stay warm.

214 ‖ VOILÀ! A FRENCH COOKBOOK

1. Wash 2 of the mandarins and grate the peels thinly. In a large bowl, whisk the butter until smooth. Keep whisking as you add the peels and the sugar. Squeeze the juice from the mandarins over the bowl and add 2 tablespoons of Grand Marnier. Refrigerate for 1 hour.

2. Spread 1 teaspoon of the butter mixture inside each crêpe. Fold them in fourths. In a crêpe pan, melt 1 tablespoon of the butter and reheat the crêpes slowly in it. In a small saucepan, heat ½ cup of Grand Marnier over medium heat.

3. Pour some warm Grand Marnier over each crêpe, tell your guests to pay attention, and light a match to flambé.

Le Petit Truc The authentic recipe for Crêpes Suzette is not "flambéd." You can eat the crêpes without this dramatic ritual or make them alcohol-free by substituting orange blossom water for the Grand Marnier.

Pairing: Pair with champagne.

CRÈME BRÛLÉE

Prep time: 15 minutes ✦ *Cook time: 1 hour and 15 minutes* ✦ *Refrigeration time: 4 hours*

VEGETARIAN · GLUTEN FREE · CLASSIC

4 egg yolks

½ cup sugar

⅓ cup brown sugar, plus more for sprinkling

1 vanilla pod, split in half lengthwise

¾ cup whole milk

SERVES 4 · Literally "burnt cream" in French, Crème Brûlée is so delicious that its name is now famous all over the world. No need to have a special blowtorch or fancy equipment—all you need is an oven, a broiler, and patience to wait for your guests to arrive before digging in.

1. Preheat the oven to 225°F.

2. In a large bowl, whisk the egg yolks with the sugars. Using a teaspoon, scrape the seeds from the vanilla pod into the bowl. Add the milk. Whisk as you slowly add the whipping cream until the mixture is homogeneous.

3. Pour mixture into 6-ounce ramekins or custard cups. Place in the oven and bake for 1 hour.

4. Take the ramekins out of the oven, let them cool at room temperature, wrap, and put them in the refrigerator for at least 4 hours.

5. Fifteen minutes before serving, preheat the oven to broil. Sprinkle brown sugar onto each ramekin. Broil for 2 minutes before serving. Take the ramekins out as soon as the sugar starts to caramelize.

Le Petit Truc You know that the custard is ready when it doesn't shake when you try to move it.

Pairing: Pair with a sweet dry wine from the Loire Valley.

CRÈME CARAMEL

CARAMEL CUSTARD

Prep time: 20 minutes ✦ Cook time: 45 minutes ✦ Refrigeration time: 12 hours

VEGETARIAN · GLUTEN FREE · CLASSIC

4 cups whole milk

1 vanilla pod, sliced in half lengthwise

1¾ cups sugar, divided

4 tablespoons water

5 large eggs

3 egg yolks

SERVES 6 · Talk about crème de la crème. This is a dessert that you must turn upside down to see the magic happen—unmold it and caramel drips down the top. Kids love *crème renversée*! And adults always fall for this dramatic dessert, too!

1. In a medium saucepan, bring the milk and the vanilla pod to a boil over medium heat. As soon as the milk boils, remove from the heat. Cover and reserve.

2. Melt ¾ cup sugar in a small saucepan with 4 tablespoons of water, over moderate heat, until the sugar gets almost golden brown. Pour the caramel immediately into 6 round ramekins of about 2 inches in diameter. Tilt them to distribute the caramel evenly.

3. Take the vanilla pod out of the saucepan, scrape the seeds out, and put the seeds back in the milk. In a medium bowl, whisk the eggs, the egg yolks and the remaining cup of sugar, until the mixture whitens. Keep whisking as you pour the milk in. Cool for 10 minutes. Pour into the ramekins.

4. Preheat your oven to 300°F.

5. Pour ⅔ inch of cold water into a large baking dish, place the ramekins in it, and cook for 45 minutes. Cover in plastic wrap. Refrigerate for 12 hours.

6. Unmold each crème on single dessert plates and eat cold.

BÛCHE DE NOËL

YULE LOG

Prep time: 20 minutes ✦ *Cook time: 5 minutes* ✦ *Refrigeration time: 24 hours*

VEGETARIAN · CLASSIC

½ cup dark chocolate

½ pound butter, diced, at room temperature

8 eggs, divided

⅔ cup powdered sugar

½ cup sugar

½ cup cornstarch

½ cup flour

SERVES 6 · "Bûche de Noël" means "Christmas log," and pastry chefs can spend hours making it look like a real wood log.

1. Preheat the oven to 400°F.

2. Prepare the cream: Fill a large saucepan with water, place over medium heat, and place a smaller saucepan on top. Add the chocolate and melt it slowly. In a large bowl, smooth the butter, whisking for 2 minutes. Keep whisking as you add 2 eggs. Add the powdered sugar and chocolate. Whisk until smooth. Reserve.

3. In the bowl of a stand mixer, whisk 6 egg whites for 1 minute at moderate speed, increase the speed as you slowly add the sugar. Whisk until fluffy.

4. In a large bowl, whisk the 6 egg yolks. Slowly add the cornstarch and the flour. Gently fold the egg whites into the batter.

5. Cover a sheet pan with parchment paper. Spread the dough all over the parchment paper, using a spoon to make sure it is evenly distributed. Cook for 5 minutes. Cover with plastic wrap. Let it cool.

6. Take the wrap off, and spread ⅔ of the chocolate cream over the whole surface. Using your hands, roll the cake into a log. Use the rest of the cream to coat the cake.

7. Refrigerate for 24 hours before serving.

GALETTE DES ROIS

KING CAKE

Prep time: 15 minutes + Cook time: 40 minutes + Refrigeration time: 1 hour

VEGETARIAN · CLASSIC

⅓ cup butter, diced,
at room temperature

1 egg

½ cup almond flour

1 tablespoon orange
blossom water

2 puff pastry sheets

⅓ cup sugar

1 egg yolk

SERVES 6 · Galette des Rois is eaten all over France during Epiphany. An almond cream tucked in two fluffy puff pastries, it's a dramatic golden dessert, with a great tradition linked to it: Each galette hides a *fève*—a tiny ceramic prize.

1. In the bowl of a stand mixer, whisk the butter and the egg. Add the sugar, the almond flour and the orange blossom water. Whisk until everything is smooth.

2. Roll out the pastry sheets. Cut out 2 large 10-inch circles in the pastry sheets. Put a sheet of parchment paper on a sheet pan and place a pastry round on it. Spread the almond cream on it, leaving 1 inch around the edge. Add the *fève* if you have one.

3. Using a pastry brush, moisten the edge with water. Cover with the second round of puff pastry. Glue the 2 pastry sheets together by pressing them and turning the tip. Using a pastry brush, brush the egg yolk all over. Use the tip of a knife to draw lines on it, in a diamond pattern. Put in the fridge for 1 hour.

4. Preheat the oven to 400°F.

5. Bake the galette for 30 minutes, then lower the heat to 350°F for 10 minutes.

6. Serve warm or chilled.

Le Petit Truc To make sure nobody is cheating to win the prize, the youngest guest should sit under the table and name who is getting each slice, one after the other! The winner must pay for or make the next galette.

Pairing: Pair with cider or champagne.

Glossary of French Terms

À la Crème: Cooked with crème fraîche.

Aïoli: A sort of garlicky mayonnaise, but also a Provençal specialty that uses the sauce.

Apéritif: A drink served before the actual meal to "stimulate the appetite," it is traditionally served alongside savory snacks and bites, and can be turned into a whole meal in itself, then called *"Apéritif dinatoire."* You can serve wine, or traditional apéritif alcohol like Pastis, Suze, or Lillet, for instance.

Apéritif Dinatoire: Drinks served with bites or munchies that actually make a whole dinner in a more relaxed, tapas-like way.

Boulangerie: A bakery. Most of the boulangeries are actually boulangerie-pâtisserie: they sell bread and pastries.

Bouquet Garni: A bundle of herbs, usually tied together with a string, or into a leek leaf, to perfume a stew for example. Usually contains bay leaf, thyme, and parsley or celery (see page 13).

Casserole: In French, a saucepan. The English word "casserole" usually means "gratin" in French.

Charcuterie: Cured and preserved meats, most of the time pork meat: ham, pâté, rillettes, saucisson. They are often served cold for an *apéritif* or appetizer, together, on the same plate. Charcuterie is also the name of the shop that only sells pork meat and cold cooked pork products.

Confit: Preserved in its own fat.

Cornichons: Small pickled gherkins, sometimes pickled with spring onions. Always serve cornichons when serving charcuterie or Pot-au-feu (page 93).

Crème Fraîche: A dairy product, crème fraîche is basically just cream—the higher-butterfat layer skimmed from the top of the milk before homogenization. It is not soured, like sour cream, and is a very common ingredient in French cooking.

Crudités: Raw salads, such as Carottes Rapées (page 55) or Concombre à la Crème (page 59), served as an appetizer.

Cuisinier: A cook.

Déjeuner: Lunch.

Digestif: A strong alcohol served in small glasses after the meal, "to help digest." It can be Calvados (apple alcohol), cognac, brandy, or *eau de vie*—alcohol made with fruit, like pear.

En Pommade: A pastry technique that consists of softening the butter until it is as soft as a face cream.

Entrée: Literally an "entrance," the *entrée* is the course that starts the meal. More like an appetizer, *entrée* is a *faux amis*—a fake friend or false cognate—with the English word, as the English word has changed its meaning over the years.

Foie Gras: A luxury food product made of the liver of a duck or goose that has been specially fattened.

Galettes: Buckwheat crêpes.

Goûter: The traditional snack kids have in the afternoon, around 4 p.m.

Gratin: A dish baked in one dish in the oven, generally vegetables. Sometimes translated as casserole.

Pâtissier: A pastry chef.

Petit Déjeuner: Breakfast.

Plat de Resistance: The main course.

Quiche: A savory open pie, usually made with an egg and cream custard.

Rémoulade: Sauce made with Mayonnaise (page 25), combined with shallots, mustard, cornichons, and capers.

Tartare: Raw meat or fish served as is. A *tartare de boeuf* is raw steak, usually mixed with various spices.

The Dirty Dozen & The Clean Fifteen

A nonprofit environmental watchdog organization called Environmental Working Group (EWG) looks at data supplied by the US Department of Agriculture (USDA) and the Food and Drug Administration (FDA) about pesticide residues. Each year it compiles a list of the best and worst pesticide loads found in commercial crops. You can use these lists to decide which fruits and vegetables to buy organic to minimize your exposure to pesticides and which produce is considered safe enough to buy conventionally. This does not mean they are pesticide-free, though, so wash these fruits and vegetables thoroughly.

DIRTY DOZEN

Apples
Celery
Cherries
Grapes
Nectarines
Peaches
Pears
Potatoes
Spinach
Strawberries
Sweet Bell Peppers
Tomatoes

In addition to the Dirty Dozen, the EWG added one type of produce contaminated with highly toxic organophosphate insecticides:

Hot peppers

CLEAN FIFTEEN

Asparagus
Avocados
Cabbage
Cantaloupes (domestic)
Cauliflower
Eggplants
Grapefruits
Honeydew
Kiwis
Mangoes
Onions
Papayas
Pineapples
Sweet Corn
Sweet Peas (frozen)

Measurement Conversions

VOLUME EQUIVALENTS (LIQUID)

US STANDARD	US STANDARD (OUNCES)	METRIC (APPROXIMATE)
2 tablespoons	1 fl. oz.	30 mL
¼ cup	2 fl. oz.	60 mL
½ cup	4 fl. oz.	120 mL
1 cup	8 fl. oz.	240 mL
1 ½ cups	12 fl. oz.	355 mL
2 cups or 1 pint	16 fl. oz.	475 mL
4 cups or 1 quart	32 fl. oz.	1 L
1 gallon	128 fl. oz.	4 L

OVEN TEMPERATURES

FAHRENHEIT (F)	CELSIUS (C) (APPROXIMATE)
250°F	120°C
300°F	150°C
325°F	165°C
350°F	180°C
375°F	190°C
400°F	200°C
425°F	220°C
450°F	230°C

VOLUME EQUIVALENTS (DRY)

US STANDARD	METRIC (APPROXIMATE)
⅛ teaspoon	0.5 mL
¼ teaspoon	1 mL
½ teaspoon	2 mL
¾ teaspoon	4 mL
1 teaspoon	5 mL
1 tablespoon	15 mL
¼ cup	59 mL
⅓ cup	79 mL
½ cup	118 mL
⅔ cup	156 mL
¾ cup	177 mL
1 cup	235 mL
2 cups or 1 pint	475 mL
3 cups	700 mL
4 cups or 1 quart	1 L

WEIGHT EQUIVALENTS

US STANDARD	METRIC (APPROXIMATE)
½ ounce	15 g
1 ounce	30 g
2 ounces	60 g
4 ounces	115 g
8 ounces	225 g
12 ounces	340 g
16 ounces or 1 pound	455 g

Recipe Index

Index